FOREWORD

"Frontiers of America" dramatizes some of the explorations and discoveries of real pioneers in simple, uncluttered text. America's spirit of adventure is seen in these early people who faced dangers and hardship blazing trails, pioneering new water routes, becoming Western heroes as well as legends, and building log forts and houses as they settled in the wilderness.

Although today's explorers and adventurers face different frontiers, the drive and spirit of these early pioneers in America's past still serve as an inspiration.

ABOUT THE AUTHOR

During her years as a teacher and reading consultant in elementary schools, Mrs. McCall developed a strong interest in the people whose pioneering spirit built our nation. When she turned to writing as a full-time occupation, this interest was the basis for much of her work. She is the author of many books and articles for children and adults, and co-author of elementary school social studies textbooks.

STALWART MEN
OF EARLY TEXAS

By Edith McCall

Illustrated by Lou Aronson

CHILDRENS PRESS, CHICAGO

Library of Congress Cataloging in
Publication Data
McCall, Edith S
    Stalwart men of early Texas.
    1. Texas—Biography—Juvenile literature.
[1. Texas—Biography]   I. Aronson, Lou,
illus.   II. Title.
F384.M22   97614'00922[920]
78-101296   ISBN 0-516-03371-9

Cover photograph courtesy
of James P. Rowan

New 1980 Edition
Copyright© 1970 by Regensteiner
Publishing Enterprises, Inc.
Printed in the United States of America.
1 2 3 4 5 6 7 8 9 10 11 12 R 87 86 85 84 83 82 81 80

CONTENTS

2114433

CABEZA DE VACA, CAPTIVE ON THE LAND   7
ESCAPE OF THE CAPTIVES   19
LA SALLE, LOST AND SHOT BY TRAITORS   39
THE AUSTINS COME TO TEXAS   64
HOUSTON, BOWIE, CROCKETT,
    TEXAS HEROES   87
LONE STAR REPUBLIC OF TEXAS   113

CABEZA DE VACA, CAPTIVE ON THE LAND

Forty men lay crowded on the rough deck of a little ship just off the Texas coast on the night of November 5, 1528. The hours dragged by. Each hour seemed a long night in itself. With every wave that hit the little thirty-three-foot ship, it groaned and creaked as if it would surely fly apart into splinters. The moon that had lighted the skies early in the night disappeared. But no man lifted his head to notice. Almost all were too sick to care. Some were even beyond hearing the groaning of the crude ship that they had built themselves, near Mobile Bay in what is now Alabama.

The wind changed. The boat shuddered more violently. Captain Cabeza de Vaca, commander of the ship, struggled to his knees, grasping the splintery toprail. Roughly, he grasped the shoulder of the helmsman, crouched over the tiller.

"Listen!" De Vaca shouted into the helmsman's ear. "Hear that sound? That's not just the wind. It is the sound of waves breaking on a shore. We'll be on the rocks before we know it!"

The helmsman swung the tiller to head the boat out to sea, and then dropped a weighted line into the water.

"Seven fathoms," he reported.

DeVaca looked out across the water to the faintly graying horizon. Dawn would soon be breaking and he would be able to see the coastline. With the water only about forty-two feet deep, they must be close to land. Whether it was a rocky coastline or a sandy beach, De Vaca had no idea. He looked at the dark forms of the men. All of them were weak from lack of food and from thirst; some were very ill from the rolling of the boat, as well. He shouted, "Man the oars!" But only two even lifted their heads. He himself seized an oar to help pull the ship away from land.

Suddenly there was a great roaring sound. The oar was wrenched from his grip. He felt the whole ship rising under him. He tried to shout as he felt himself flying through the air, but he could not. Blackness, then, and blankness.

Not long afterward De Vaca awoke to find himself still in the boat. But the ship was still, no longer tossed about on the waves. It had been lifted by a giant wave and set onto a sandbar. By some miracle, not one man had been thrown into the sea. Now they were crawling from the boat onto the beach, the first Europeans on Texas soil. DeVaca, too, climbed out and dropped to the sand.

As he lay there panting, his first thoughts were of thankfulness that his men had been delivered from the sea. They were all members of an exploring party that had known nothing but bad luck in the year and a half since leaving Spain. There had been six hundred in the company, led by Panfílo de Narváez, sailing in June of 1527 in five fleet Spanish caravels. Narváez had planned to explore the land between Florida and Mexico and begin several settlements along the shore of the Gulf of Mexico. Narváez was sure he could do better than had Ponce de León, killed in 1521 by Florida Indians when he tried to start a settlement.

"That will not happen to me, your Majesty," he told the King of Spain when he asked for ships and men. Narváez had helped conquer Cuba in 1511, and had lost an eye in Mexico in a conflict with Cortez. As a reward for his service, King Charles had given Florida to Narváez.

Cabeza de Vaca was treasurer for Narváez' expedition, and second in command over the men. Now lying on the beach, he remembered with bitterness what had happened to Narváez' grand plans. At the first stop on the island of Santo Domingo, 140 men had deserted. Going towards Cuba, the six ships had been scattered by a hurricane, and sixty men and one ship had been lost. The four hundred remaining men spent the winter months in Cuba, sailing for Florida in the spring. The five ships probably had anchored in what is Tampa Bay, on the west coast of Florida, in April. Narváez took most of the men on foot from there, while small crews took the ships along the coast of the Gulf of Mexico. The men were going by land to find gold.

DeVaca clenched his fists, forcing the white sand between his fingers as he remembered that long march. It seemed like a nightmare now. There had been Indian battles in which some of the men were killed. The hardtack they carried for food had not lasted long, nor had the bacon. The last of the bacon had spoiled, but they had eaten it anyway. Sick and hungry, the men marched inland because Narváez was sure they would find gold. They had found none—only the gold of pumpkins and dried corn stolen from the bark and pole huts of Indian villages. At last they headed back to the coast to get supplies from the ships. But day after day passed and not one ship was seen.

Narváez finally ordered the men to build ships. There were about two hundred men still alive, and they had five horses left from the two dozen or so they had brought from Spain. While the men worked, the horses kept them alive, for one was killed every three days for food. They melted all the bits of metal they could find, including stirrups and spurs, to make nails, saws and other tools. Pine trees furnished lumber and pitch to seal the seams between the boards. Ropes were made from the tails and manes of the horses. Shirts became sail material. Forty men died while they worked. Indians killed ten more who went on a food-hunting trip beyond the camp. But after many days of hard work, there were five little ships. The last horse had been eaten.

Narváez appointed a leader for each boat and divided the men into groups of from forty-seven to forty-nine. DeVaca was one of the captains. On September 22, the little fleet had headed westward to try to follow the gulf coast to Mexico. Thirst brought a problem in just a day or two. Each boat had a water bottle made of the hide of a horse, but the bottles leaked and rotted, for the hides had not been properly tanned. To go ashore for fresh water was to take the chance of running the ships aground. They watched for a river mouth and saw the Mississippi. But a strong north wind blew them away from shore and, with their poor little ships, they could not get into the river to get fresh water. The winds brought bad storms and the ships were separated. That was the last that De Vaca had seen of any of the other boats.

Now, lying on the beach at dawn on that November day, De Vaca shuddered. A cold north wind was swooping down upon the men. He got to his feet and saw that four others already were standing. The helmsman had walked to the top of a gentle rise and was waving his arm for the others to come.

"There is shelter here," he called.

DeVaca went to the top of the rise. From there he could see a little hollow, edged with wind-bent shrubs. Soon, all the men were in the little ravine, and those who could walk were gathering driftwood and twigs from the bushes for a fire. DeVaca went back to the boat and found that the last of their food, a sack of dried corn, was still there. If they only had water, they could make the corn into cakes or gruel.

"Halloo! Halloo!" he heard faintly above the wind, and saw the adventurous helmsman again pointing to something. He had found a pool of rainwater. Soon every man who was strong enough was on his knees beside the pool, bending over to drink. DeVaca stayed on his knees long enough to say a prayer of thanks. Then he went to the boat for the wooden bucket one of the men had made, and took water to the weakest of the men. Before long, all of them were feeling better.

DeVaca walked back to the ship. It was deep in the sand and the wind was piling more sand around it. But by some miracle there did not seem to be much damage. An hour or so of work and the ship could be afloat again. They could go on their way to Mexico. Or perhaps it would be better to travel by land if they were near enough to Mexico. He must learn what he could of their location.

"Oviedo!" he called to one of the stronger men. "Climb that tree and tell me what you see."

Oviedo pulled himself up the trunk until he was in the swaying upper part of a lone pine tree at the end of the ravine. Soon he was back down.

"We are on an island, Captain," he reported. "I could see a shallow lagoon not far beyond the ravine, and then more land beyond the lagoon. It appears to be gentle country, were it not for this infernal wind. But just over yonder, on this island, I saw more trees and I am sure there were huts of an Indian village."

"Go there," said De Vaca. "Take this knife as a gift for their chief and get us some food."

Oviedo set off, climbing a gentle ridge and then dropping from sight. When he had not returned in fifteen minutes, De Vaca sent two more men to find him. They called from the top of the ridge, "Here he comes! But there are three Indians a little way behind him. He seems to be trying to make them follow him here."

Oviedo appeared at the top of the ridge, carrying a clay pot in which the men soon saw there were some fish. He turned and waved a beckoning arm to the three Indians before he came down the slope. After a few minutes, the Indians appeared at the top of the ridge, but they would come no nearer. They sat down there as if awaiting something or someone. DeVaca became a little uneasy.

"Oviedo," he asked, "what are they waiting for?"

"I don't think they ever saw any people other than Indians before in all their lives," Oviedo said. "They are afraid of us."

They soon learned what the Indians were waiting for. Suddenly, silhouetted against the sky, on the top of the

ridge, there were about one hundred men armed with bows and arrows. DeVaca jumped to his feet, motioning his men to be quiet and stay back. He walked towards the Indians. Soon one of them also came forward.

He was a big man, with powerful muscles. As he drew near, Cabeza de Vaca saw that he and all his warriors were tanned to a deep bronze, and that they all had holes in their upper lips with a piece of cane run through the holes. DeVaca motioned that he came in peace, and the chief waved a signal back to his warriors. Just the same, they remained ready to draw their bowstrings, with arrows in place.

"Oviedo!" DeVaca called back to his trusted helper, who stood ready to come to the aid of his leader if one arrow were let fly. "Bring gifts for our new friends."

The chief saw the bright cloth, the glittery mirrors, and the metal hatchets. He heard the tinkling bells that Cabeza de Vaca's men brought to him. He called back to his warriors to lower their arrows. Then he sent a few of his men for the best food they had to offer the hungry explorers, some roots and more fish.

"We will stay just long enough for our men to be stronger," said Cabeza to the Indian chief, making him understand through signs. "Then we shall sail away again in our boat and leave you, our new friends."

A few days later, he gave the chief a fine cape he had had admired and said good-bye. The men put all their belongings and a supply of food and drinking water into the little ship.

"Strip off your clothes and put them into the boat." Cabeza ordered the men. "We'll have to push her out into deep water before we go on board."

The men already had dug away the sand that half buried the little craft. Now, naked and shivering, they pushed and lifted until at last they had the boat afloat. Swimming alongside and pushing it, the forty men moved it out into open water. They scrambled aboard and seized the oars to keep the boat from being washed back onto the sandbar. The wind had come up stronger in the last minutes of their struggle, and the men were blue with cold, but there was no time to get into their dry clothing.

The helmsman shouted, "Hold on, men! A big wave coming!"

The men leaned hard on the oars. DeVaca turned and saw the great wave, rising higher than the deck of the ship. On it came, a wall of water, with another and even greater wave following not far behind it.

The first wave washed over the deck and several men fell. DeVaca saw the next one drawing nearer, felt the ship rock and rise.

"Each man for himself!" he shouted.

This time the ship was not carried safely to a sandbar. With one last shudder, it broke into bits.

This land that someday would be called Texas (from the Indian word *Tejas* meaning "friendly people") was not going to let these Spaniards leave.

ESCAPE OF THE CAPTIVES

Thirty-seven men huddled together in the same ravine that had sheltered them before. They were not only captives of the land. They were naked. Three who had tried to hold onto the ship had drowned. Those who had reached shore dug into the sand to keep warm.

There the Indians found them once more. They formed a circle around the shipwrecked men and began to sing. To the Spaniards, it sounded more like the howling of dogs than like music. After about half an hour of this, the Indians led the shivering men to their village, took them inside the smoky little round huts, wrapped them in robes, and let them warm themselves around the fires.

The Indians danced in joy all night. Now the Spaniards had less than the Indians themselves. They had lost the magic of their guns and metal swords. They were prisoners. As prisoners they would be slaves of their Indian captors.

Two days later, Cabeza and Oviedo, with an Indian guard, walked back to the beach to see if any of their belongings had washed ashore. They found only a few planks.

"I don't know how we'll ever get to Mexico now," said Cabeza. "They won't let us just walk away, and even if we did, we couldn't go far in this winter weather without food."

They pulled their buffalo robes closer about them as they turned to climb back up the ridge. At the top, Oviedo turned to look back up the beach and something caught his eye.

"Look, Sire!" he cried, grasping Cabeza's arm. Cabeza turned. Oviedo's voice carried excitement and new hope. "Those must be some of our men from another of the ships!"

The Indian guard turned and ran back towards the village. Here were more of the strangers. And these had guns and swords. Cabeza and Oviedo ran to greet their friends. Soon they learned that the newcomers' ship had been forced ashore just a little way up the beach. It was not badly damaged.

"We'll make it to Mexico, then," said Cabeza.

Among the new arrivals was the strongest man of the whole company. He was Estavan, a north African black who had been sold to the Spanish as a slave. He towered

above the Indians as well as the Spaniards. Estavan led in the work of getting the boat repaired, and it was he whose strength gave it the last push it needed to set it afloat. The men loaded all their goods onto it, and the crews of both ships climbed aboard. They shoved off into deep water. They waved farewell to the Indians as the wind filled the patchwork sails.

But something was wrong.

"She's sinking fast!" one of the men shouted. They just had time to leap from the boat as it sank beneath them. Their hope of escape went to the bottom with their boat. Again the Indians took them in, and again the Spaniards faced the fact that without the Indians' help, they could not live through the winter. They chose four of their strongest men, all good swimmers so that they would be able to cross the rivers, and sent them as messengers to try to reach the Spanish settlements in Mexico.

The Indians seemed to know that the men would not be able to live many days. They gave them some food and allowed them to leave. But the men were never heard of again.

It was a terrible winter. The island was swept by storm after storm, and the Indians could catch no fish.

Hunger deepened into starvation, and one man after another died, Indians and Spanish alike. More than eighty Spaniards had come to the little island, but before that winter of horror ended, there were only sixteen left.

"We'll call this place *Malhado*—Bad Luck Island," Cabeza said. "I wonder if any of us will ever get away." He and Oviedo and Estavan were among those who were alive. Sometimes they thought they would go mad, however, listening to the wailing of the Indians hour after hour, as they carried on funeral ceremonies for their dead. Cabeza noticed that the Indians tried to save a life by blowing into the lungs of the person who was ill.

"Do the same," the chief ordered Cabeza de Vaca. "Use your magic to drive out the illness and make our people well." The Indians were suffering not only from starvation, but also from some strange new disease, probably brought to them by the Spaniards.

Cabeza shook his head. "We have no magic. We cannot make your people well."

To his surprise, Cabeza saw that the chief was angry.

"He thinks we don't want to help," he decided. He was sure of this when the chief sent no food to the captives the next day.

"No food until you use your magic to make my people well," the chief said.

Cabeza was worried, for they had no medicine with them, nor did they know what might cure the sick Indians.

"It would be better to try than to starve to death," said Castillo, one of the men who had come through the winter in better health than most. Castillo's father was a physician.

He and several others went to the hut of a sick Indian. Cabeza knelt beside the man, said a prayer, and then leaned over and breathed into the sick man's mouth. He and the other Spaniards said some of the prayers used in the churches in Spain, and Cabeza added a special prayer for the health of the Indians. Then they moved on to another hut, doing the same things over and over until they had visited all the sick Indians. Castillo told the chief the sick men should also be fed some of the liquid left from boiling a certain root.

To the surprise of the Spaniards, some of the sick Indians were up and walking about the next day.

"You saved them," the chief said. From that time on, Cabeza was put in a special position in the village, honored as a medicine man. The Indians took him across the lagoon to the mainland to go to another Indian village to use his magic with the people there.

Cabeza himself became ill while he was in the villages on the mainland. When his fever left, he found that the Texas meadows had come alive with blue wildflowers. Warm breezes promised summer would soon be there.

"I want to go back to my friends," he said, and soon he was back at the island village. He saw no white men moving about among the huts. None worked in the swamps where the Indians dug the roots that they used for winter food. He looked about for the tall figure of Estavan, but he was not there. He looked inside the huts. At last he saw a face of a friend. Oviedo, looking very pale as if he were just recovering from an illness, was lying on a robe while two Indian women fed him.

"I'm the only one left, Sire," Oviedo told him. "Thirteen left a few days ago to try to find their way to Mexico. Alaniz and I were too ill to go. Alaniz died, and I am alone now."

Cabeza shook his head sadly. From the little he had seen of the land, those thirteen men would have a hard time trying to get food for such a long journey. If they were not captured by Indians, they would starve to death. He would go to Mexico, too. But not until he found a way to travel in safety.

The next months were the hardest of Cabeza's life. He was ordered to work for the Indians, mostly at digging roots from under the water in the swamps. The sharp, broken reeds cut his bare feet. His fingers were so sore that they were raw and bleeding. In the warm weather, the Indians wore almost no clothing, and he had to do the same. The hot sun burned and blistered his tender skin over and over again.

"Anything would be better than this," he finally decided. "I've got to make my plans now."

An idea came to him when an Indian from an inland tribe came to the seashore villages and greatly admired the shells that could be picked up along the beach. Cabeza pulled Spanish moss from a tree and twisted and knotted the fibers to make a net bag. He filled the great sack with the choicest of shells that he could find and a supply of the best roots. Without telling the chief what he was about to do, he slipped away from the village one day. After a few days' journey inland, he found a tribe that admired his shells and liked the flavor of his roots when he showed them how they were used. They traded lumps of clay, called ocher, that was used to make a

good yellow paint, and chunks of flint that could be shaped into arrowheads or knives.

Then he went back to the seashore. He was welcomed back with his ocher and flint.

"Through being a trader, I can move about to learn more of the nature of the country," he decided. And it was most certainly a better life than root digging in the swamps! As soon as he could fill his nets, he set out again. He was also called upon to cure people when illness came, and for some reason he was more often successful than not.

Four years went by.

"The time has come," he decided. He went to the island settlement where Oviedo was living just as the Indians did, with his two women to wait on him. Oviedo was not anxious to start out, as he had learned to live quite comfortably. But at last Cabeza was able to talk him into leaving Bad Luck Island. Oviedo could not swim, but Cabeza promised to help him across the rivers. The two Indian women insisted that they would go where their "master" went, and the four set out.

They followed along the coast, going southwest. No one is quite sure of their exact route, but they had crossed four large rivers when they met some Indians who had seen some other Spaniards. "Three men," they told Oviedo and Cabeza. When asked if there hadn't been more, they shook their heads.

Cabeza questioned them some more, and then said, "Let's make camp here. They claim that three men are being brought here as prisoners."

"How soon?" asked Oviedo.

"They don't know. Maybe a day or two, maybe longer."

It was harvest time for a kind of nut that grew plentifully on trees along the riverbank where the two men and the Indian women camped. The Indians from other villages were there to gather the ripened nuts. They came to see the two strangers. They poked them. They slapped them to see if they would cry out or pull back. They pressed arrows against the Europeans' chests to test them further.

"Tomorrow we come to kill you," they threatened.

Oviedo believed them. He told Cabeza he was going back to Bad Luck Island while he could still walk and where he could live in peace. Cabeza pleaded with him, but in the dark of the night Oviedo and his two women set out for the island. Cabeza never heard of him again.

Two days later, he was working with the Indians, filling a clay pot with nuts, when he heard a cry.

"Sire!" He turned and saw three of his old companions. There was a man named Dorantes, Castillo, the physician's son, and Estavan, towering above all the other men. Cabeza almost spilled all the nuts he had picked in his haste to grasp the hands of his old friends. There were tears in the eyes of each of the four.

"Where are the other nine?" Cabeza asked.

"All dead," Castillo answered. "Some died of illness and some of torture after we were all captured four years ago."

In the night, they whispered together of how they could escape from the Indians. Cabeza was now a fourth captive of the traveling Indians.

"We must not try right now," he told the others. "But I know what we can do in the spring. Winter is coming too soon now. We will stay with this tribe until it is over." He told them of his trading journeys and how he could be welcomed by the tribes as he went from place to place if he planned it well.

Through the winter, the four men did as they were ordered, working without complaint. Spring's gentler breezes came in February, and Castillo wanted to start out.

Cabeza reminded him of what had happened to him

and the others four years earlier. "We want to have a good chance to get all the way to Mexico." He told them then that this tribe would be going to the prickly pear cactus grounds in early summer. Then the yellow cactus blossoms of early spring would have developed into a purple fruit that the Indians called "tuna."

"There will be tribes that know me at the tuna grounds, and who will help us along our way," Cabeza said. "We will go with this tribe to the tuna grounds, but that is the last they will see of us."

They were impatient for the time to pass, but tried not to show it. They pretended to accept the life they were leading as slaves. They had long ago learned to eat spiders, worms, caterpillars, lizards, snakes and ant eggs, as the Indians did through the months when fish and roots were hard to get. But they welcomed the time when the Indians formed a great circle of dry grass and then lighted it to force all small animals to move to the center of the circle. The meat was a pleasant change. The warriors did nothing but kill the game. All the labor was done by the women and the four captives.

At last the time came to leave the camp near the coast. They all headed inland going to a place about where Austin, Texas, is today. But the four captives had a terrible disappointment. Before they had a chance to get away, their captors quarreled with the other tribes and decided to leave in the night, taking their useful captives with them.

The four men waited another year. This time they slipped away from the tuna grounds in the light of a full moon. Within an hour they came to the camp of a tribe that remembered Cabeza from his trading days. These Indians were called the Avavares, and remembered that Cabeza had healing "magic."

"We have men in need of you," the chief said. "Come."

Soon the four were praying over Indians who had terrible pains in their heads. Within an hour, each of the men declared his headache was gone.

"Stay with us for a feast," the chief said. The four not only stayed on with the Avavares for a feast, but journeyed southward with them and spent the winter in their village. As healers, the men were treated well, but Cabeza remembered it as a difficult time because of having no clothing. His skin would peel under the Mexican sun. "The sun and the air made great sores on our chests and backs," he wrote later, "which pained us much because of the large, heavy loads which we carried. Often, after we brought wood from the thickets, blood ran from our bodies in many places."

He liked the days on which the Indians gave him a hide to scrape, because he could sit quietly scraping, and would eat the bits of flesh he scraped off the hide. By summer, this was all that was left of the buffalo brought down when the herds came to winter on the Texas grasslands. Cabeza wrote the first description Europeans ever read of the American bison or buffalo, comparing the animals with Spanish cattle.

One day, Cabeza was called to heal a man who had been brought to the village seeming to be more dead than alive. He prayed until he was exhausted. The man seemed to be breathing more easily, and Cabeza dozed. When he awoke, the sick man was half sitting, sipping broth that Castillo had shown the women how to make.

The chief was amazed. "Truly you are a child of the sun," he said. From that day forward the four of them were honored. They were taken from one village to the next, with much wailing by the people they were leaving and singing from the people who welcomed them to their villages. All through the summer of 153£ the Children of the Sun traveled across Texas, honored and feasted wherever they went. Sometimes three or four thousand Indians traveled with them.

"Sometimes I wish we were not quite so honored," Cabeza sighed. Wherever they went, they had to go through great ceremonies. He wrote, "As we had to breathe upon and sanctify the food and drink for each, and grant permission to do the many things they would come to ask, it may be seen how great was the annoyance."

They reached the southern ranges of the Rocky Mountains, and were told that desert lay beyond the mountains, and enemies to the northwest. "You must stay with us, Child of the Sun," the chief told Cabeza when he asked for guides to help them find a safe passage.

Cabeza shook his head. He could not give up now. "We must go on," he said, "and we will need guides to show us the way."

The chief refused. Cabeza took his mat from the lodge where he slept and walked towards the woods. "I shall sleep apart from your people, since you are no longer my friends," he said. Castillo, Dorantes, and Estavan went with him to the woods, where they cut poles and built a hut. They slept there that night. In the morning, a messenger stood waiting as they came outside.

"Our chief begs you to return," he said. "Two of our people fell ill in the night."   2114433

Cabeza said, "Tell your chief that the Children of the Sun will return to heal his people only if he promises to show us the way to the northern villages."

In an hour, the man was back. "The chief begs you to come now. There are five who cannot rise."

"Does he grant us our request?"

The messenger said, "He cannot do that. He says we will all die if you leave."

Cabeza turned his back. "Let them die here if they will not take the Children of the Sun to the northern people."

That night, the four men heard wailing and cries from the village. In the morning they learned that half the people of the town were sick, and that eight had died. The chief himself came to them this time.

"It is our punishment," he said. "We have denied the request of the Children of the Sun. I beg you not to wish death upon my people. We will take you to the land of our enemies. Only stop the sweep of death among my people."

All four went back to the village. They used all the knowledge they had of how to treat the sick people, and had those that were ill separated from the others to stop the spread of the illness. Then they prayed earnestly for help in saving the lives of the Indians. No more died, and in a few days there were only two Indians too sick to be up and around.

"I believe that our Lord wants us to find our way across this land and back to our own people," Cabeza said. "He has performed so many miracles to help us on our way."

And so they left Texas and journeyed on, seeing the pueblos of the Indians of the Southwest, and their patches of corn and squash and beans. At last there was plenty of food for the travelers. The Indians also gave them gifts of chunks of fine turquoise, and one very special offering of five arrowheads shaped from an emerald.

It was the spring of 1536 when they reached the shores of the Pacific Ocean, the first men to have journeyed from the Atlantic waters to those of the Pacific in North America.

One day, Castillo saw an Indian who wore a strange ornament hanging from a necklace. It was a Spanish swordbelt buckle with a horseshoe attached to it.

"Where did you get these?" Gastillo asked.

The Indian answered that they were left by men who wore beards like those of the four travelers. Castillo could scarcely wait for more information. Where had the men gone? To the land of the sinking sun, on ships, he was told.

From then on, the men knew they were drawing near to Spanish settlements as they moved to the south. They did not hear much that was good of the Spaniards, however. They learned of Indians forced into slavery or killed, of corn burned in the fields in which it was growing, of robberies of the storehouses of the Indian farmers. These things disturbed Cabeza, Castillo, Dorantes and Estavan, but their own good reputation helped them to travel in safety. They were given guides and guards for their journey all the way south to Mexico City.

The stories that they told of the Texas lands led to armies of men traveling there, armor glinting under the sun as the men followed their leaders who rode horses with fine silver ornamants on their bridles and saddle skirts. Castillo and Dorantes wanted no more of overland journeys and stayed in Mexico City. Cabeza de Vaca was an important man in Spanish government, and after he had told his story of years in Texas, he returned to Spain. He was soon back in the New World as governor of Paraguay, in South America.

It was the giant black Estavan who went back to the lands to the north and east of Mexico, showing the way for the Spanish soldiers who carried the red and gold banners of Spain into Texas. Estavan himself was killed by the Indians in the pueblo country, leading Coronado's men in a search for cities of gold, the Seven Cities they believed were there.

The only gold they found was "fool's gold" or mica, gleaming in the sun. But Cabeza's stories of Texas made them want to hold that land just the same.

In the next hundred years, the Spanish began to build a scattering of small forts and Indian mission stations to hold the land. They were disturbed when they heard that explorers from another country said Texas belonged to them. A clash was sure to come.

LA SALLE LOST, AND SHOT BY TRAITORS

The quiet of the bayou country around the mouth of the Mississippi River was broken by a new sound on an April day, a hundred-fifty-four years after Cabeza de Vaca had landed in Texas. No one but a few Indians had disturbed the rule of the alligators in the swamps and the wildcats on the land, for more than a hundred years. The new sound must have made the creatures of the wilderness tremble and scurry into hiding.

"Boom! Boom! Boom!" About twenty big-muzzled guns were fired, re-loaded, and fired again and again. Before the last boom's echo had died, the wild creatures heard another strange sound. Human voices rose in a shout, "Long live the King!"

The men who caused all this disturbance were gathered around a tall column they had set into the ground. It was on a rise of land on the Mississippi River delta. Their leader, Robert La Salle, stood with his plumed hat in his hand and his head bowed as the men sang a hymn in praise of God. God had been good, indeed. Now, after years of struggle, LaSalle's dream of reaching the mouth of the Mississippi River had come true. He and his men had journeyed southward from the French settlements around the Great Lakes, down the Illinois River to the Mississippi and all the way to the great river's mouth. La Salle raised his eyes to the tall column on which were carved words claiming this land, and all the land that the great river drained, for France. It was 1682.

Again the men were digging into the loose, rich black soil. This time they placed a great cross into the hole they dug and piled the earth back around its base. The cross was to honor God. The men thanked Him for their safe arrival.

They buried a heavy lead plate, then, and sang a hymn. When the hymn was ended, they shouted again, "Long live the king!" and the ceremony was ended. France, far across the ocean, now claimed almost all the land between the Rocky Mountains and the Appalachians. This included much of the land that Spain was saying belonged to her.

"We will be back," La Salle told his good friend, Tonty of the Iron Hand, who stood beside him. "We will be back to build a great French city to guard the mouth of the Mississippi River."

It was two years before La Salle could get back to try to build that settlement. But in April of 1684, three little wooden ships, carrying about a hundred soldiers and a hundred people to start a colony, entered the Gulf of Mexico. Now at last they were nearing the end of their journey. La Salle's orders were to drive the Spanish back toward Mexico beyond the Rio Grande River, as well as to build the new colony at the mouth of the Mississippi.

The three ships, the *Aimable,* the *Joly* and the *Belle* had rounded the Florida peninsula and now were headed westward in the Gulf of Mexico. La Salle, on the leading ship, the *Aimable,* was on deck, always on guard for any Spanish ships they might meet. Two of his young nephews were with him, as well as one of his brothers, Jean Cavelier, who was a priest. Another who had come on the trip was Joutel, the son of the gardener on the La Salle estate in France.

La Salle scanned the horizon with his telescope. His younger nephew, who was only fourteen, asked, "How soon, Uncle? How soon do we reach the Mississippi?"

"Three days, perhaps," said La Salle. "Or it may be a little more. We are following the twenty-eighth parallel, and we should be heading directly toward the river delta."

"But what longitude?" asked his other nephew, Moranget. "Surely you know how far west we should go."

La Salle shook his head. "I had no instruments to measure the longitude when we came down the Mississippi by canoe. We can only watch for land and the inlets of the delta."

But the ships were a little south of the delta land. The *Aimable* passed the Mississippi River mouth with no one realizing it. When, on the twenty-eighth of December, a sailor on watch called out "Land, ho!" they had gone almost to the Texas shore.

The welcome cry brought all hands to the deck. The shoreline grew clearer each minute. The *Aimable* headed into a bay, making sure that the *Joly* and the *Belle* were following.

"Our settlement will be about sixty miles inland, where the land rises and is dry," La Salle told his people. So the ships moved slowly along, with everyone watching for higher land. All they saw was marshland and sand. On New Year's Day they saw higher land, and went ashore. But La Salle soon decided this was not the place. Neither was the next bay that they entered. There was fog for a while, and then a storm that kept

them all at work trying to keep the ships from being washed ashore and wrecked.

Then, at last, when the storms ended, La Salle saw land that looked better to him. It was the entrance to Matagorda Bay, about halfway between today's cities of Galveston and Corpus Christi.

"This is it!" he announced. The ships threaded their way into a narrow passage between sandbars and a small island known today as Pelican Island. All but the sailing crews went ashore to begin the work of building shelters and finding a supply of water. La Salle ordered the ships brought into the inner harbor to be anchored safely.

"Tow them in," he ordered. "Don't try to come in under sail. You'll go aground on a sandbar."

The *Joly* and the *Belle* were soon safely anchored, but the captain of the *Aimable* was not obeying La Salle's orders. He sped along under full sail. La Salle, watching from the shore, was worried.

"Fools," he muttered. "They'll run aground."

He shouted, but he could not make himself heard. Between his calls to the crew of the *Aimable*, he heard someone calling his own name. He turned and saw two of his men who had been cutting down a big tree to hollow out and shape into a canoe. They were waving and shouting.

"Indians! Indians are attacking!" they yelled.

La Salle ran towards them. "They took some of our men and dragged them away," the frightened men explained.

"Take up your arms and come with me," La Salle said. He was not alarmed. He had had plenty of experience in dealing with Indians and was sure this problem could be settled easily. What really worried him was the danger to the *Aimable*. He looked back once more and shook his head in despair. Then, taking his musket and sword, he led the way in the direction the men pointed.

The Indian town was not far away. There were about fifty huts in it, shaped like upside-down cups, covered with mats and hides. The Indians stood watching as La Salle and his men came near.

Just as he reached the edge of the village and raised his right arm, there was a great BOOM! La Salle knew it was from the guns of the *Aimable*, being fired as a distress signal, and he knew that what he had feared had happened. But the Indians had never heard such a sound before. They dropped to the ground in terror.

La Salle stepped over them, striding from lodge to lodge until he found the chief.

When he and his men left a little later, they had the captives with them. They also had gifts of buffalo meat and dried porpoise meat. La Salle hurried on to see what had happened to the *Aimable*.

"Just as I feared!" he said when he saw the ship. She was on her side, hopelessly aground. The little rowboat that the *Aimable* towed was smashed, and La Salle shouted orders to get a boat from the *Joly*. There were two Indian canoes of the hollowed-log type that could also be borrowed. La Salle shouted orders and all men at hand pitched in to the work of getting the cargo from the *Aimable* moved to the shore.

They had taken some barrels of gunpowder and flour to the beach when La Salle noticed a sudden gathering of black clouds, pushed toward the little camp by strong winds.

"Hurry! A storm is coming!" he shouted.

But his warning was of no use. The waves rose so that the men could not move the small boats against them to get back to the ship. There was no choice but to seek shelter until the storm's fury was over.

When they could return to the shore, they saw that

the *Aimable* had broken up. Waves had washed into the hold, tossing the bales and boxes and casks about until they, too, had split apart. Only a few washed ashore unbroken. The men stacked all the goods that had been saved on the beach until a proper storehouse could be built.

Dusk came soon after the storm ended. The men went to their tents and pole huts to prepare an evening meal and get some rest. But rest time had not yet come, for one man saw moving forms on the beach.

"Indians are stealing our goods!" he shouted.

Quickly, La Salle sent men with loaded rifles to the shore. The Indians had disappeared into the woods, but La Salle had the drums beaten to call all men to assemble. He divided them into groups and set a time for each group to go on guard duty, until all the goods were safely stored. During the long night, more storms came.

When he checked what had come ashore and compared it with the *Aimable's* cargo list, La Salle found that they had lost a great deal. Seeing how discouraged his leader looked, young Joutel asked La Salle, "What can I do to help, Sire?"

La Salle's face, handsome but becoming lined with cares and worries, lighted up at the question. "There are so many who seem to be doing all they can *not* to help that just hearing you ask does my heart good," he said. "But there is one thing I wish you would help me with, Joutel. Help me to know who can be trusted. There are some who would shoot me in the back given the chance, I am sure."

"Oh, no! That could never be," said Joutel.

La Salle turned away from the sea and put his arm on the young man's shoulder. "When you have journeyed in the wilderness as long as I have with some of these fellows who hire out as soldiers or workmen, you will know that it is all too true. There already have been those who tried to kill me. But not such as you and my good friend Tonty. Someday you must meet him."

"I hope that someday I shall," Joutel said. "For now, let me take his place as much as I can."

La Salle felt that here was a young man he could truly trust. He gave him much responsibility in the days that followed. They moved to a better building site, farther inland on the banks of the Lavaca River. While the work of planting a garden and putting up a few buildings went on, the *Joly* sailed for France. La Salle sent word back to the men on the last of his ships, the *Belle*, to bring it up to a safe harbor near the new settlement.

The *Belle* belonged to La Salle personally, a gift from the King of France. He watched each day for it to arrive, but the *Belle*'s crew had disobeyed orders and sailed for home. It was never seen again. All the goods still aboard the ship disappeared with it.

This was a terrible blow to La Salle. There were other troubles, too. The garden withered under the hot sun. No rains came. The strongest of the men, led by Joutel, were weary from dragging logs from the nearest grove of trees, three miles distant. Illness struck. Thirty people were buried in a little graveyard just outside Fort St. Louis, as La Salle had named his settlement. By the middle of summer, La Salle realized that this could not possibly be the Mississippi River delta. He said nothing, but he noticed there was much grumbling, and more and more often, groups of people stopped talking as he came near. "Are there some I should not trust?" he asked Joutel.

Joutel said, "They do not talk against you when I am near, but I would keep an eye on that fellow who used to be a pirate, Hiens. Then there is that quiet one, Duhaut. There is something going on in his mind, I am sure, something he is planning to do if things don't get better soon."

The next day La Salle told Joutel he had decided upon some action. "We came here to drive back the Spaniards. That is why the soldiers are here. But I planned on two or three thousand Indians to make up most of my army. I must go back to the Mississippi River lands to find the warriors I know will be willing to help push back the Spanish. The main part of the river can't be more than a few miles from here."

So La Salle, with his brother, Father Jean, and fifty soldiers, left Fort St. Louis. Joutel was in charge while they were gone. They left in the fall, and Joutel expected them back in a month or two. But winter came and went, and they had not returned. Neither did a ship come from France with supplies.

By the end of March, the people were becoming very unhappy. Joutel noticed that more and more often, Hiens and Duhaut were in the center of little groups, talking in low voices. They always switched to a new topic if he came near. He, too, was growing discouraged and worried. Then one day when he was repairing a roof he saw some men walking slowly toward Fort St. Louis. Joutel could count eight men in the party.

He climbed down from the roof and called out to a group of men working in a field just beyond the fort wall, "Get your guns and come along. Company is coming!"

La Salle's young nephew asked, "Could it be my uncles and the soldiers returning?"

Joutel shook his head. "I don't think so. But perhaps they bring word from La Salle."

Cautiously, they walked out to meet the travelers. Joutel stared at the man who led the tired-looking little group. From the way he walked, he was sure it must be Robert Cavelier de La Salle! But his clothing was ragged and his beard had grown scraggly. La Salle had never allowed this to happen in all his years in the wilderness. And that tattered figure beside him must be Father Jean, but his robe was in shreds. Joutel wrote later, "There was hardly a piece left large enough to wrap a farthing's worth of salt. He had an old cap on his head, having lost his hat by the way. The rest were in no better plight, for their shirts were all in rags. Some of them carried loads of meat, because Monsieur de La Salle was afraid that we might not have killed any buffalo. We met with great joy and many embraces."

They sat together later, eating bread and drinking brandy while a buffalo roast was cooking. Joutel asked the question that had been on the tip of his tongue since La Salle's arrival. "Did you find it, Sire? Did you find the Mississippi River?"

La Salle shook his head. "I thought we had found it. We built a small fort on the shore of a wide waterway, but I fear now it was not the Mississippi."

Duhaut, Hiens and a few others got up from the table and walked away. The company's surgeon, Liotot, arose to leave, too.

Another man asked, "And what of the rest of the company that went with you? Are they in the new fort you built?"

"They died in Indian battles and of illness," La Salle said. His voice sounded harsh, but Joutel knew he was just covering his own sadness. He reached out to touch his leader, who seemed so stern and forbidding to most of those who worked for him. Like Tonty, Joutel could see the greatness of this man who would not let his dreams die.

La Salle could not rise from his mat the next day. For weeks, he was too ill to know what was happening. But on April 22, he got ready to leave the fort again. He was going up to the Illinois forts to get supplies for the settlement, or all the way to Canada if necessary.

"We will all die if I do not get the help my people

need," he told Joutel. "Help me prepare for the journey."

Joutel took his own clothing from his chest for one of the men to wear who was going on the journey. The chests of those who had died were opened, and their clothing taken to help the living. Again, Father Jean would go with his brother. Their nephew, Moranget, another priest named Father Douay, and sixteen of the other men were chosen to go. With packs on their backs, including gifts for the Indians, the men set out, anxiously watched by those who were staying behind.

But again after a few months they were back. They had hacked their way through thick masses of canes taller than any of them, with La Salle leading the way as usual. There had been many hardships. Nika, La Salle's faithful Indian hunter who had journeyed all over America's heartland with La Salle, nearly died of a rattlesnake bite. All had to use their wits to keep from being murdered in the night by Indians who pretended friendship in the daytime. La Salle and Father Jean had been swept away by floodwaters on a raft and had nearly drowned before they reached shore. They had lost one man to a ferocious alligator. Again, La Salle had been ill with a high fever, unable to travel for weeks. Moranget was also ill. While they were sick, eleven of the men deserted the camp. There was no choice but to return to Fort St. Louis, again eight in number.

Gloom hung over the settlement as the last months of 1686 dragged by. Christmas came, and the priests said Mass before a rough little altar. On Twelfth Night, La Salle announced he was ready to leave again.

He had bought five Spanish horses from Indians who had got them on raids into New Mexico. These were loaded with supplies for the travelers. But La Salle was taking different people this time, except for a few. Moranget, Father Jean, and Father Douay were going again, and of course the Indian hunter, Nika, was to go. La Salle's younger nephew, now seventeen years old, had begged to go along and was allowed to. La Salle also decided that Liotot should go along so that there would be help for those who were injured or sick. He thought it best to include some of the most discontented, too, for fear they would destroy the settlement if he left them behind. So he took Hiens and Duhaut, and two friends of theirs, Teissier and DeMarle. There were a few others, and at the last minute La Salle made another decision.

"Joutel, I want you with me this time. Perhaps our luck will change," he said.

There was another parting, and the men headed into the woods, leading their five packhorses. In a few days the deerskin moccasins they had made when their boots were no longer wearable also wore out. They met a herd of buffalo and Nika brought down several of them. After they had taken the best meat to carry with them on the packhorses, the men cut new moccasins from the raw buffalo hide. But the untreated leather shrank in the daytime, hurting their feet, and grew stiff at night. They had to keep the hides wet in order to be able to walk at all. At last they were able to buy some tanned deerskins from Indians, and made new moccasins.

They came to the Brazos River, followed long ago by Cabeza de Vaca, and made a buffalo-hide boat for the crossing. They carried the boat with them and used it for other river crossings. They crossed the Trinity River, and went on to the northeast.

They were not far from the Red River that is now the boundary between Texas and Oklahoma when bad weather forced them to stay in camp for four or five days. Joutel noticed Liotot, Hiens and Duhaut often talking together in low voices, away from the others.

Joutel went to La Salle. "I am not so sure you should have brought that little group along, Sire," he said. "While you were on your last journey, I heard Duhaut talking against you. He blames you for the death of his brother, who left with you on that first journey and did not come back."

La Salle said, "He was ill and could not go on. I sent him back to Fort St. Louis with a few others, believing it to be best for him."

"I know," said Joutel. "The others told us that, and that the man was killed by Indians. It was the fault of no one. But Duhaut grumbled against you, just the same."

"We'll keep an eye on him and his friends," La Salle agreed. Then he saw how worried Joutel looked. "Do not be afraid for me, my friend. More than one man has tried to kill me, but I am charmed, for I have important work to do. I have eyes in the back of my head to see those cowards who would strike from behind." He smiled, and Joutel returned the smile.

They moved on. On the fifteenth of March, they were camped only a few miles from a place where La Salle remembered having hidden a supply of Indian corn and beans on his last trip. He sent Duhaut, Hiens and

Liotot, along with Duhaut's servant, Archeveque, to find the food. Joutel raised his eyebrows at La Salle's choice of men to go on the errand, and La Salle added, "Nika and Saget, you will also go." Saget had worked for La Salle for many years, and he was as loyal as Nika.

A few hours later in the day, Saget returned alone with a message. "We found the corn and beans, but they had rotted in the hole in the ground in which you stored them," he reported. "But Nika saw buffalo as we were returning, and killed two of them. He asks now that you send some horses to bring in the meat."

The sun was already setting. "Rest for the night, Saget," La Salle said. "You would only get lost in the darkness returning to their camp. In the morning, Moranget and DeMarle will go with you."

The three set out in the morning. When they reached the camp, they found that Duhaut and the others had started to smoke the meat, so that it would keep better. As was usually done by those who butchered wild meat, they had set aside certain choice pieces for themselves.

Moranget had a quick temper. "What makes you think you have the right to the best meat that my uncle's hunter found for all of us?" he asked angrily. As he spoke he reached for a choice marrow bone with tender meat on it. Duhaut jumped up to take it back, and Moranget struck him a hard blow in the jaw. Liotot and Hiens rushed in to pull Moranget back. The young man turned about, fists flying, and knocked down Liotot. Nika and Saget pulled Moranget back with DeMarle's help.

Liotot said, "What kind of man are you, Moranget? Have you forgotten that I nursed you back to health after you were struck down by that Indian's arrow? Have you no gratitude?"

Moranget's only answer was a string of curses.

DeMarle was shocked. "Sire, your uncle would not handle the matter in that way. These men had a right to that meat. Nika did not mind if they took the choice pieces. Certainly the matter is not worth coming to blows over."

Moranget muttered something and walked away into the woods alone.

In the meantime, Duhaut and Liotot, each with a swelling eye from Moranget's fist, were talking together off to one side. They returned to the group some time later.

Duhaut had been put in charge of the party by La Salle. "Since we are staying the night to finish smoking the meat, I will assign guard duty. Moranget, you take the first hour. Second, Saget, and the third hour is yours, Nika. DeMarle, you take the fourth hour, and Archeveque and Teissier after that. Each man arouse the next man.''

The evening meal was finished and darkness closed in except for the glow of the fires. Moranget finished his hour on guard and awoke Saget. Soon Moranget was asleep, wrapped in his blanket. Saget finished his tour of duty and awakened Nika. The Indian, too, completed his rounds and then aroused the sleeping DeMarle to take over. Nika was soon asleep.

While DeMarle was facing away from them, Duhaut and Hiens arose silently and stood facing DeMarle, guns held ready to be fired. Liotot, ax in hand, walked over to Moranget. He dealt one blow and quickly moved to Saget and Nika in turn. These two made scarcely a sound and lay still, but Moranget sat up, struggling to call for help. DeMarle swung about, horrified to see the blood streaming from the lifeless men and Moranget.

The other two men, Teissier and Archeveque watched in silence, for they had been told of the murder plot. DeMarle faced the two rifles pointed at him and heard Liotot say, "You finish off Moranget, DeMarle.

Then you'll be as guilty as we are." The surgeon handed DeMarle a knife.

"It's murder! I can't do it," he said.

"You can and you will unless you choose to die with them," Liotot said, and DeMarle did as ordered.

La Salle watched all day for Moranget and the others to return, not knowing they had decided to smoke the meat at the other camp. As evening came, he would have gone to look for them, but he did not know where they were camped. At nightfall, he was told that one of a group of Indians who had come to the camp knew where the others were.

"In the morning, take me to them and I will give you a new hatchet," he told the Indian.

La Salle could not fall asleep. "Joutel," he whispered, "did you hear Duhaut and Liotot talking of any plans?"

Joutel whispered, "Nothing special. Just more complaining about your never being satisfied with what they did, Sire. Of course, they know better than to talk of plots in my hearing."

"I had thought to have you go with me in the morning, Joutel," La Salle said, "but I believe it would be better if you stay here and keep a careful watch. I have a feeling that there is something very wrong."

When the black of night gave way to the first gray of dawn, La Salle roused Father Douay to go with him and the Indian guide. As they walked along, Father Douay was surprised to hear the usually quiet and calm La Salle talking in a rather nervous manner. He spoke of the way that God had cared for him during his many years of adventure in America, bringing him through one time of danger after another.

"Don't you feel that He is watching over me so that I may complete my work for France in His Name?" he asked. He grasped the friar's arm.

Father Douay looked at his leader sharply. He had never seen La Salle so disturbed.

"Of course, of course," he said. "Let me say a prayer to help you believe."

After the prayer, La Salle seemed his usual self. The Indian guide stopped at last and pointed across a shallow stream. "There," he said.

La Salle fired his pistol into the air as a signal of their approach. Soon he saw Archeveque standing on the opposite bank.

"Where is Moranget?" called La Salle.

"Around somewhere," Archeveque replied in a careless tone.

La Salle said sharply, "Speak to me with respect and answer my question properly." He sloshed his way across the stream.

"Now, lead the way and quickly," he ordered.

Archeveque just stood there and laughed. "I'm in no hurry, so why should you be?" he said.

La Salle's temper flashed, and he struck out at Archeveque's mouth with the back of his hand. But at that moment a shot rang out, followed by another. Duhaut and Liotot, crouching in the long grass, had done their work. La Salle, the great explorer, the man with the dream of a great French empire, lay dead on Texas soil.

The murderers fled into the woods. In due time, the news of the assassination of La Salle reached Tonty of the Iron Hand, at La Salle's Illinois forts. Tonty journeyed to Texas when he heard that Duhaut was living there with Indians. He did not find him or Liotot, either in Texas or in Arkansas where he went later on the trail of revenge.

The people at Fort St. Louis struggled on a little longer. But when the Spanish, hearing of the French settlement in Texas, came marching to the Lavaca, they learned their journey had been needless. All they found were a few logs and bits of debris, and the bleached bones of the last of the French people of Fort St. Louis.

THE AUSTINS COME TO TEXAS

Things were rather quiet in Texas for the next one hundred years or so. Now and then the French would advance into Texas from the settlements that they finally built near the mouth of the Mississippi. Then the Spanish would send soldiers marching up *El Camino Real,* The King's Highway. They would come from Mexico to the Rio Grande. Crossing that river, they would head eastward to the mission and fort at San Antonio de Bexar. Then they would go on to Nacogdoches, the Texas settlement farthest east. From there they would go wherever the rumors said the French had been seen. But very few Spaniards came to Texas to build homes. Even the mission stations were often left with only one or two priests to manage them.

After 1763, the Spanish no longer had to worry about the French trying to take their land. Following the French and Indian War, the whole Louisiana Territory became Spanish. A Spanish governor came to the old French settlement of New Orleans.

So Texas lay almost empty, all through the 1700s. But

when the 1800s began, things were about to happen and to happen quickly. Americans began to see a new frontier in Texas.

Far away to the east, in the Appalachian foothills in southwestern Virginia, there was a man named Moses Austin. He had opened some lead mines and started a new town for the people who came to work for him. He had done well in operating the mines, and had built the first lead rolling mills in America. Before coming to Virginia, he had been in business in Connecticut and Pennsylvania. But by 1796 most of the lead was gone from his Virginia mines.

"It's no use beating a dead horse, Maria," he told his wife. "It is time to move on."

Maria Austin turned from stirring soup in the kettle that hung in the fireplace. "Moses Austin, we're just beginning to get this place civilized. Now where do you want to go."

Moses crossed his legs as he sat in the fine Windsor chair the Austins had brought from their earlier homes to the frontier. Instantly, little three-year-old Stephen Fuller Austin seated himself on his father's foot for his daily "pony ride." His black eyes sparkled as Moses Austin reached out for the boy's hands and began the game. The little boy, who had the same deepset eyes and wavy brown hair as his father, had been born there in the little Virginia lead-mining settlement. "Spittin' image of his father," people said, "and just as smart, too."

Mrs. Austin went over to the little cradle where baby Emily was sleeping. For a moment or two she rocked the cradle with her back turned to her husband. When she turned around, she was smiling. "Where will it be this time?" she asked.

Moses lifted Stephen to his lap. "You'll like it, Maria. We will be living among French and Spanish people, in the Missouri part of the Louisiana lands. I have heard that the French opened some lead mines there about sixty years ago. But no one has operated them for about fifty years. Now, my plan is to leave right away and go to look the place over."

And so, during that winter of 1796-1797, Moses Austin went far to the west, to the Spanish land of Louisiana. He found the old mines just south and a little west of St. Louis, a French fur-trading settlement. There seemed to be plenty of lead left, and it could be shipped to market by river to New Orleans. Moses

Austin went there to talk with the Spanish governor about his plans.

He called his people together when he reached home. "We must agree to become Spanish citizens," he told them. "But the governor made me feel that we would be welcome. The Spanish government wants people to come to develop the lands. Are you willing to go with me?" From the cheer that arose, he knew that most of his workers would be on hand to open the Missouri mines. He had a land grant of about three square miles.

Immediately, the men began building flatboats. In a few months, the fleet was moving down New River. The boats were loaded with mining equipment, tools, household goods, a few animals, and, of course, the families who were going to Missouri with Moses Austin. The New River joined the Kanawha that flowed into the Ohio River. Down they went, past new little settlements. But along the Illinois shore there were no settlements at all, and there was danger from Indian attack. They reached the Mississippi safely, however, and turned upriver. It was difficult poling the boats, and so they crossed to the Missouri shore to finish the journey by land.

Soon there was activity at the old mines such as the

people of the little French villages nearby had never before seen. Before many months had passed, furnaces were melting the first lead taken from the ground. Moses Austin was again in full swing as a successful businessman.

Through all the hard work of turning Indian hunting grounds into a center of industry, little Stephen was at his father's heels, learning all he could. The years passed. There was a little brother, James, to watch over, and school lessons to be learned. In 1803, there was great news. The land on which they lived had become French territory again for a few months, and then was bought by the United States. Automatically, the Austins and their neighbors became American citizens once more.

Stephen would have liked to see the boats that Captains Meriwether Lewis and William Clark were taking up the Missouri River. But when the explorers started out from St. Louis, Stephen was in Connecticut in school. He was still away when news came of the return of Zebulon Pike from another exploration journey, a little farther south.

"Pretty clever of Captain Pike," Moses Austin remarked, reading from the St. Louis newspaper while

Maria sat with her sewing. "You know he was captured by the Spanish when he went down into New Mexico after he reached the western mountains. The Spanish held him prisoner for a while, and then brought him all the way back to Louisiana under guard. They would not let him take notes or draw maps of their land. Do you know what he did? He jotted down important notes and hid them in his boots!

"Now he's written a report on his trip across Texas. He says it is dry in the west, but nice country in the east. He says he was glad to see green trees when he came near San Antonio de Bexar, where the Spanish government offices are."

He put down the paper, and sat gazing dreamily into the fire. After a few minutes, he said, "You know, Maria, I'd like to look over that land down there in Texas. I hear that a few Americans have already gone there to live."

"Surely you wouldn't leave these mines, Moses. They are doing so well," said Maria.

Moses laughed then and said, "Don't worry, my dear. I won't uproot us again without good reason."

But "good reason" came some years later. Stephen, grown to young manhood was back in Missouri, and already had begun to explore lands farther west. He became a land owner in Arkansas. Moses Austin had done so well with his mines that he was able to invest a great deal of money in the new Bank of St. Louis that opened in 1816. But he soon became concerned over the condition of business in the United States. Western lands were opening fast. "Too fast," Moses remarked. "People are buying land on credit or with paper money printed by banks with no real cash."

Moses was right, and in 1818 one bank after another closed its doors, its funds gone. The Bank of St. Louis was among them. Moses Austin, who had never before made a bad business deal, was angry with a government that would let this happen. His money had almost all been lost.

"Maria," he said to his wife, "we left the United States to live under the Spanish government once before. We are about to do it again. We'll go to Texas, and we'll take all the people who want to go with us and start over again."

Maria was silent a moment. Then she said, gently, "My dear husband, we are growing old. You are now fifty-seven. Do you realize how it will be to go once again into a wilderness to live? Have you forgotten all we went through in Virginia and here? I ask only because I love you, and want you with me many years more."

Moses Austin turned to the window as his wife spoke. His shoulders sagged a little as he looked out at all he had built in twenty years of hard work. Yes, it had been difficult, and he was growing older—but old? No! His shoulders straightened as he turned back to Maria.

"We shall go to Texas," he said. "Stephen is young, and he will carry much of the load. He can start right away getting plans made to move our people. There's plenty of empty land in Texas, and I am sure the Spanish government will welcome us again with a large land grant."

Mrs. Austin nodded. Yes, they had Stephen to count on. Emily was married, and James was away at school. But Stephen was like a younger Moses. They could count on him. Yet, as Moses prepared to go on a journey to Texas, she felt a weight pressing down about her. She could not shake it off.

Out in Arkansas, Stephen was soon gathering families on his land on the Red River, getting ready to lead them to Texas. He was impatient to start, and was delighted, on a day in the fall of 1820, to see a familiar figure come riding down the trail from Missouri.

"Father!" he called.

"I'm on my way at last, Stephen," said Moses Austin.

Stephen motioned toward his camplike settlement. "Should I spread the word for the people to get ready to go?"

"No, no! Not so fast, young man," Moses Austin said. "We must have legal rights for these people to go to Texas. The Spanish must welcome us. If we went down without a land grant, they might think we are another such group as that fellow Magee led into Texas in 1812."

"I remember reading about that," Stephen said. "He was going to take Texas away from the Spanish. Seems to me he and his men were nearly all killed or taken prisoner, weren't they?"

Moses nodded. "Now I am on my way to San Antonio de Bexar to ask the governor for a land grant for our people. We will let him know that we do not want to steal Texas, but to become good Spanish citizens."

It was agreed, before Moses left, that Stephen would soon go to New Orleans to get more people for the colony, and to get two ships ready to take heavy supplies by water.

"I'll send you word as soon as the papers are made out," Moses Austin said and headed down the lonely rough trail that led to Nacogdoches, Texas. Mile after mile, he saw unbroken grasslands with a few groves of oak trees, and cottonwoods growing along the streams. He passed an old mission, almost in ruins, and an Indian village nearby. On he went, a little nearer to Nacogdoches each day. It was a journey of about 180 miles. From there, it was almost twice again as far to San Antonio de Bexar.

About halfway between the two settlements, Moses Austin saw land that he thought would be fine for his colony. It was along the Brazos River, about 125 miles from the river's mouth. He hurried on towards the capital, the sooner to be able to lead his people to this beautiful land.

At last he was in Bexar and talking to the governor. But the governor was in no mood even to read Moses Austin's plan for starting a colony. There had been an American attempt to take Texas. The leader was Dr. James Long of Natchez, Mississippi. Long had been captured by Spanish soldiers and was now in prison in Mexico City.

Austin explained that he intended to be a good

Spanish citizen. "We will obey Spanish laws," he said. "We will bring farming tools, build homes, and plant the land."

"No, no, no!" the governor said. "I have orders from Mexico City to admit no more foreigners to Texas. Especially no more Americans!"

Moses tried again to show him how his plan would make Texas stronger. But the governor turned away. He was having a difficult time keeping the Spanish government strong. There had been a revolution in Mexico ten years earlier, led by a priest, Father Hidalgo. He believed Mexico should be a free country, independent of Spain. Father Hidalgo's punishment for leading the revolution had been death. But the spirit of freedom had not died with him. Now the Spanish government was trying to put down another revolution. There were troubles enough without letting any more of these Americans into Texas to stir up the Mexicans with talk of independence.

"Just go," he told Moses Austin. "Leave Texas right away. I shall put you in prison if you do not obey my order."

Moses Austin turned away. He dreaded the long journey back to Missouri with only bad news to carry. But

he had orders to leave. He would shake the dust of San Antonio de Bexar from his clothes that very evening. But even as he made up his mind to go, Moses Austin felt a terrible weariness come over him.

As he walked across the plaza to get his horse and begin his journey, he knew he was not well enough to start out. "I should find a place to spend the night and start in the morning," he thought. He raised his head to look about for an inn. His eyes met those of a man coming toward him. Both men stopped, and then hurried toward each other.

"Baron? Baron de Bastrop!" said Moses.

The other man was smiling and holding his hand out in welcome. "Mr. Austin! It is a long time since we talked together back in New Orleans. What brings you to Bexar?"

"It is a long story and a sad one, now that it is ended," said Moses.

"Then you must come with me to my room and tell me all about it, old friend," the Baron said. "It is only one poor room, and I wish I had more to offer. But you do not look well. You must come with me."

Soon Moses was in the Baron's room telling him the whole story. The Baron had known trouble in his own life and was a good listener. He had come to America from Europe because of trouble there, had become a Spanish citizen in Louisiana, lost his money when the United States bought Louisiana, and then gone to Texas to live.

He said now, "But my good friend, what you want to do would be the best thing that could happen to Texas! It is wrong that you should not be allowed to do it. You must go back to the governor and talk to him again."

Moses shook his head. "It would do no good. He ordered me, over and over again, to leave Texas as fast as I could reach the border. He would put me in prison if I showed up again tomorrow."

"You are not leaving today," the Baron said. "You look ill. You will stay with me for the night."

In the morning, Moses Austin could not rise from his friend's bed.

"Stay here," the Baron said. "I will be back in a short time."

He went to the governor's palace. Soon he was back. "Moses, you are to remain here until you are well enough to travel. I told the governor he would be responsible for your death if he forced you to travel today."

For a week, Moses stayed in Baron de Bastrop's room, but the Baron was not there with him during many of the daylight hours. He was a well-liked and respected man in Bexar, and he talked to many people of Austin's plan during that week. He spent hours with the governor.

At the end of the week, the Baron had good news. "Moses, you shall yet lead your people to Texas!" he cried as he returned to his room. "The governor has at last sent a recommendation to the Mexican government that you be granted permission to follow your plans, leading three hundred families to your colony. You are to have free choice of the place where your grant will be."

It was the best medicine Moses Austin could possibly have had. The next day he seemed his old self again. "It will take weeks or even months for the papers to be completed," he told the Baron. "My family will be concerned, and I must start back now. I will not forget all I owe you, my dear friend."

The Baron promised to send a messenger with the papers as soon as they arrived. So Moses Austin started on his homeward journey. He planned to go home by a different route, through Natchitoches in Louisiana.

From there he could send word to Stephen down in New Orleans that there would be some delay.

He rode eastward, through Nacogdoches, toward the Sabine River. Beyond Nacogdoches, the trail led through woods and swamps. Heavy rains came and made traveling difficult. His supply of cornmeal and dried meat ran out. He planned to shoot small game for food, but his rifle would not fire. Water had seeped into his powder horn. Coughing from a bad cold, he struggled along the trail with almost nothing to eat for eight days.

Outside his cabin just across the Sabine River, at the shallow-water trail crossing, settler Hugh McGuffin saw a rider coming. As he watched, the man slumped over and almost fell from his horse. Running forward, McGuffin kept Moses Austin from falling off as the horse climbed the riverbank.

"This man is very ill," McGuffin told his wife, as he helped Austin from his horse. Mrs. McGuffin went into the cabin and smoothed the rough sheet on the bed in the corner. Her husband brought the traveler, almost unconscious, into the room. For three weeks, Moses Austin lay on the McGuffin's bed.

"I thought he was crazy," Hugh McGuffin said later.

"He talked of leading his people to the Promised Land—seemed to think he was Moses of the Bible."

Moses Austin had been in the McGuffin cabin about two weeks when one day a young man pounded on the door.

"My uncle—Moses Austin—I was told he might be the sick man you have here," the young man said when Hugh opened the door. "I am Elias Bates, his nephew. I came from Missouri to look for him because Mrs. Austin was so worried."

McGuffin held out his hand. "You are a most welcome visitor. We were concerned about your uncle starting from here alone. Now you can take care of him and see that he gets home all right."

When Elias had been with him a week, Moses seemed strong enough to start out, and they rode horseback to Natchitoches on the Red River. There they took a steamboat to the Mississippi, and another steamboat northward to the landing nearest Herculaneum, Missouri, where Moses had built his lead mining and smelting works.

Moses Austin seemed to be better for a while, but the cough hung on. In June, when he wanted to start south again, he became very ill with pneumonia. On June 10,

1821, Maria listened closely, as Moses seemed to want to tell her something important.

"Tell Stephen to take the people to Texas," he said. He died later that day.

Down in New Orleans, Stephen had taken a job working in a newspaper office when he received his father's letter telling him of the delay. He used his spare time to study law with an old friend who had become a New Orleans attorney. But Stephen's mind was mostly on the Texas plans. He had arranged for the two ships that would sail from New Orleans to Galveston Bay, and he had interested many families in going to the Texas colony. He was impatient for word from his father, and watched each day for a message. But instead of a letter from his father, in May he received word that Spanish officers had arrived in Natchitoches, with papers to be signed for a land grant in Texas.

"I'm on my way at last, Joe," he told his attorney friend. "Father is probably on the way to Natchitoches, too. I'll send word, and we'll look for you to open the first law office in our new settlement."

Stephen boarded a steamboat and went up the Mississippi to the Red River, where he changed to a smaller boat for the trip to Natchitoches. He wasted no time in locating the Spanish officers there.

"We expected to meet your father here," the Spanish gentlemen said. "We sent word to him at his home that we would be here. He was to go with us to·San Antonio de Bexar to sign the documents and swear his allegiance to Spain."

"I don't understand why he hasn't come," Stephen said.

The officials said they could wait no longer.

"Then let me take my father's place. I am his partner in forming the colony."

They set out on the trail to Nacogdoches. At the Sabine River crossing, they stopped at Hugh McGuffin's cabin.

"Mr. Moses Austin was here in December and January," McGuffin told them. "But he was so ill that we were worried about him, even when your cousin came to help him home. Can you tell me if he made his journey safely?"

"Yes," said Stephen, "and he wrote me of your great help to him. We are most grateful to you and Mrs. McGuffin. We expected him to be with us now, and if he should come along in a day or so, we hope you will tell him we are on our way to Bexar."

They left. The next day, a messenger from Missouri arrived at the McGuffin cabin, looking for Stephen Austin.

"He can't be very far down the trail," McGuffin told the messenger. "Good news, I hope?"

But it was news of his father's death that the messenger took to Stephen. "But Stephen, almost his last words were that you should not let anything interfere with getting the Texas colony started," the messenger said when Stephen was about to turn back to Missouri.

It was a difficult time for Stephen. He sent word to his mother that he would do as his father had asked, and rode on. At San Antonio, the deeds were completed and changed to his own name.

Stephen Fuller Austin spent the rest of his life building and managing a great colony in the heart of Texas, taking many hundreds of families there in spite of great difficulties.

First, the two ships he had sent with heavy tools and supplies and a few families were lost off Galveston Bay. They ran into storms there as the Spanish ships had done so many years before. Then Stephen was told that his land grant was not good, for Mexico had won its independence and the new government did not honor the work of the old. As soon as he could, Stephen left his settlers and headed for Mexico City alone on horseback.

Along the way, a band of Indians suddenly surrounded him. They took his horse and everything but the clothes he wore and left him to die of starvation. Stephen was by no means willing to do this. He caught a wild horse and rode bareback to Monterrey. There he made friends with a man who agreed to ride with him to Mexico City. The two dressed like poor Mexicans and said they were going to the capital to get pay owed them for serving in the army of the revolution.

When he arrived in the Mexican capital at last, Stephen Austin talked with the heads of the new government. But before anything was settled, there was another revolution, and new men took control. Stephen had to convince them. It took weeks and weeks. But at last his papers were approved, and his land grant was made large enough to take care of six hundred families instead of three hundred.

Back home, Baron de Bastrop helped him in issuing the land titles. Each family could have a league of land, which was about 4,428 acres, for only $200. By 1825, the Austin colony had a population of 4,000, all people who worked hard to develop farms on the land between the Brazos and Colorado rivers. Stephen F. Austin was their leader in everything. He wrote a constitution and set up a government for the colony, with its capital in a new little settlement on the Brazos River, called San Felipe de Austin.

Austin settled Indian troubles, acted as judge in quarrels among his people, and was business manager and adviser to all. He spent most of his time on horseback, riding from place to place in his colony. He had no time to marry and have a family of his own, for he was "father" to all his people. In time, he earned the name, "Father of Texas."

HOUSTON, BOWIE, CROCKETT
TEXAS HEROES

"Let's go to Texas!"

Young men in the United States heard of rolling grass lands where the buffalo came in great herds to spend the winter. They heard of wild cattle to be had for the catching, and of bands of wild horses that ran with manes and tails streaming in the wind.

Stephen F. Austin's advertising booklets reported Texas soil was fertile and the climate usually gentle. In 1825, the new Mexican government urged Americans to come to Texas to help build up the land, and become Mexican citizens. Although Austin's colony was the largest, several other colonies were begun in east-central Texas as Americans flooded into the open lands.

Among the thousands of Americans who went to Texas in the next five years were several who would later be remembered as heroes. One of them was Samuel Houston. Another was Jim Bowie. A third was Davy Crockett.

Sam Houston would become a great leader in Texas, but his family wouldn't have believed it possible when he was a boy. The only thing they might have believed he would lead was a move to get out of work.

"Laziest boy I ever saw! He just doesn't seem to belong in Major Sam Houston's family," people said when Sam was a lad of ten in Virginia.

When Sam was thirteen, in 1806, his family moved to the frontier Tennessee settlements. Sam's father had bought four-hundred-nineteen acres of land in Tennessee, planning to take his family there. He died suddenly, but Mrs. Houston decided it was best for her and the nine children to go to Tennessee anyway. She bought a Conestoga wagon, packed the household goods into it, and off they went.

Young Sam certainly wasn't the weakest one of the family, even if he was good at getting out of hard work. He was as tall as any of his five older brothers, "three axe handles high." There was lots to be done on the frontier to develop a new farm, but Sam did so little of it that his mother decided to apprentice him to the storekeeper in town. But he often got out of that work. He made friends with Cherokee Indians who lived nearby, and would disappear for days at a time, and live with the Indians. They adopted him into their tribe and named him *Co-lon-neh,* The Raven. Sam was sent to school and became a frontier schoolteacher in a subscription school. But he tired of this, too, and away he went to the Cherokees, this time to stay for many months, until the War of 1812 had begun.

Sam enlisted in General Andrew Jackson's Tennessee militia and was sent to take part in the battle against the Creek Indians in Alabama. He was leading a platoon in the battle when he was struck in the shoulder. The bullet became deeply lodged and he was sent home to recover. But when he was well enough he went back into service as a lieutenant. While he was still in the army, one of his tasks was to see that his old friends, the Cherokee Indians, were moved from their lands in Georgia and Tennessee to the distant lands west of the Mississippi, in what is now Oklahoma.

Sam studied law next, in Lebanon, Tennessee, and he seemed to have found the right work at last. He ran for political office, and by 1823 had been elected to Congress. Four years later, when he was thirty-four years old, he became governor of Tennessee. General Jackson, also from Tennessee, had become President Andrew Jackson, and he believed that Sam Houston might be the next man from Tennessee to become President of the United States.

But in 1829, Sam Houston again ran off to join the Cherokee Indians, leaving the office of governor to do so. He had been a bachelor until January of that year, when at last he had taken a bride to live with him in the Tennessee governor's mansion. Only a few weeks later, the bride left her new husband. Samuel Houston never explained why this happened. He just packed up some clothing and a few other things and headed west to Oklahoma to the Cherokee reservation.

He was just across the border from Texas and now and then rode into that Spanish land. Many Americans now were saying that Texas ought to be part of the United States. President Andrew Jackson sent an offer of five million dollars to Mexico as a purchase price for Texas. But his offer was refused just as quickly as had been the offer of former President John Quincy Adams, of two million dollars.

Soon there were rumors that the former Tennessee governor was planning to lead the Cherokees into Texas and seize the country from the Mexicans. President Jackson heard the rumors, and wrote to Sam, "It has been communicated to me...that you had declared you would, in less than two years, be emperor of that country by conquest." Jackson asked Houston to send his word that he had no such plans. Houston did so.

Sam, living with the Cherokees, decided that the United States Indian agents were not being honest with the Indians. He went to Washington to speak before Congress for the Cherokees. As he sat in the gallery of the House of Representatives, Sam heard one of the congressmen call him a dishonest man. He stopped the man on Pennsylvania Avenue and beat him with a hickory cane he had brought from the Tennessee woods. The congressman brought the case to a hearing before the House of Representatives. When the hearing ended, Sam Houston was back in good standing.

"But Sam," President Jackson said to him afterwards, "How could you talk about the American flag as *your* flag as you did in court?"

"It is *my* flag," said Sam.

"Then put your life in the service of that flag," said the President. "Work in the West for the United States, not just for the Cherokees."

Sam headed west again. But this time he went to Texas, arriving in Nacogdoches in December, 1832. By that time, the Mexican government had ordered that no more Americans were to come to Texas. There were ten thousand American-Texans by 1830 when the order

had been given, and not nearly that many Mexican-Texans. The order, however, did not keep other Americans out of Texas any more than it had stopped Sam Houston from coming.

Sam was told, "Most of the newcomers are from your own state. So many of them have come that the route through the lower Sabine River country is known as the Tennessee Trail."

Houston left Nacogdoches after a while and went to San Felipe de Austin. There he met some of the leaders, but not Stephen Austin. Austin had just left to ride again to Mexico City to try to get separate Mexican state government for Texas. Then Sam rode on another two hundred miles to San Antonio de Bexar. There he met the famous Texan, Jim Bowie. Before Sam returned to Nacogdoches to open a law office, he had learned a great deal about Texas and about how the people who lived there felt.

When he got back, he went to the most popular place in Nacogdoches, Brown's Tavern. It was a gathering place for Americans, and they were all talking about the latest news. General Antonio López de Santa Anna had led another revolution, and now he was the head of a military government in Mexico.

"Now we'll never get our own state government," one of the men said. "Mr. Austin's trip to Mexico City will be a wild goose chase. Santa Anna isn't going to listen to him."

Another man spoke up. "There's just one thing for us to do, and that's fight for independence from Mexico."

In the months that followed, the fight began. Stephen Austin was held in prison in Mexico City by Santa Anna, who said he had plans to lead the Texans in revolution. When at last Austin was allowed to return to Texas, he, too, was ready to see Texas try to become independent. Sam Houston was asked to be commander-in-chief of an army of volunteers who were ready to fight to make Texas free.

Jim Bowie was a restless sort of fellow, always traveling about on his horse, and as big and handsome as Sam Houston. He had been in and out of Texas for several years. Almost everyone knew him, or had heard stories of him and his brothers. But two years before Sam Houston met him, Jim had settled down in San Antonio de Bexar. He had become a citizen of Mexico.

Early in December, 1830, he was riding up the trail

that connected Texas and Arkansas. He rode into the little settlement of Washington, Arkansas, just north of the Red River, and went directly to the blacksmith and metal-working shop.

"Mr. Black!" he called. In a moment, James Black came from the back of his shop where he did the final work on the knives for which he was famous. His knives took and kept a keen edge. They were so well balanced that they seemed almost a part of the owners' hands.

Black smiled as he saw who awaited him outside his shop. Jim Bowie was dressed as usual in plain dark clothes of fine material and perfect tailoring. His boots were of the best black leather. He got off his horse and turned around. When he took off his hat, the sun brought red glints to hair that had once been light but now was darkening. It was plain to see that a good barber had tended Jim Bowie's hair, and had trimmed the long sideburns that were coming into fashion. Jim's features were fine-drawn, with keen gray eyes, rather deep-set, a long nose, and well-shaped mouth and chin.

"Glad to see you, Jim," said the smith. "Are you on your way up to your brother Rezin's place, or heading back down to Texas?"

Jim said, "I'm on my way to Rezin's plantation, Mr.

Black, but I'll soon be going back to Texas. Did you know I'm about to marry the loveliest Spanish lady you ever saw?"

The two men chatted awhile. Black always enjoyed a chance to talk with Jim Bowie, who at thirty-four was already a legend. Tales, some true and some not true, were told of duels he had fought, of how he always helped the weaker man in a fight, of his great courage. He was half rough frontiersman and half gentleman, one of a large family from Louisiana, just across the Mississippi from Natchez.

There, in the country where the cypress trees with their giant roots or "knees" grew up out of the swamp water, the Bowie boys learned how to live in the wilderness. Jim liked to trap bears by taking a big hollow cypress knee, putting honey into the bottom of the hollow, and ringing the top of the opening with spikes bent downward and inward. The bear would put his head into the trap to get the honey, and the spikes would prevent his pulling it out. While the bear thrashed around, young Jim would take his hunting knife and plunge it deep into the trapped animal's chest or throat.

When the Bowie boys were young men, three of them, John, Rezin and Jim, were very close. They met the famous pirate and smuggler, Jean Lafitte, in New Orleans. They worked out a deal to help Lafitte smuggle black slaves into the United States from Lafitte's headquarters on Galveston Island. All three of the Bowies became wealthy through this smuggling trade, and then through dealing in land sales. Rezin and John settled down to managing their plantation and taking part in Arkansas and Louisiana politics. But Jim was off to one adventure after another. He had a quick, temper, and seemed to be always in some kind of trouble, but he usually came out on top. A great deal of his success was due to his skill with a knife. He didn't slash out in the heat of anger, however. He once said, "I never fight when angry, gentlemen." In those days, when people fought duels, the fights were arranged ahead of time, as a matter of settling a dispute.

In the 1820s, Jim had begun buying Texas land and selling it at a profit. As he went about Texas, people began to know him and to tell stories about him. One of the favorites was of the day that Jim Bowie was riding through the plantations in Louisiana, near his home. When he saw a man whipping a black slave who was tied to a tree, Jim Bowie got off his horse, walked over to the tree and cut the ropes with his knife, while the slaveowner stood with his whip raised and his mouth open in surprise. Then the man dropped his whip and drew his pistol. At close range, he pulled the trigger, but the pistol failed to fire. Bowie, with one quick movement of his knife, slashed the man's wrist and the pistol fell to the earth. Then, the story went, Bowie took his own neckerchief to slow the flow of blood, helped the man to a place behind him on his horse, and rode with him to the nearest doctor.

James Black, the maker of knives, waited to see why Jim Bowie came to call on him.

"Look, Mr. Black," said Jim, "I've whittled a wooden pattern for the knife I want you to make me. If you will make it while I am at Rezin's plantation, I can pick it up on my way back to Texas, in about four weeks."

"I'll have the finest knife you ever handled ready for you," James Black promised, and Bowie mounted his horse and rode on.

When Bowie returned, Black had two knives ready for him.

"This one is from your pattern, but here's another I'd like you to try," Black said. "Take whichever one you want."

Both knives were single-edged, with a guard to protect the user's hand, but Black's own design had been sharpened along the curve back from the point as well as on the long edge. Bowie chose Black's design, which became famous as the Bowie knife.

Jim headed back into Texas with his new knife, early in 1831. Waiting for him along the trail were three men who had been hired to kill him by one of Bowie's enemies. They rushed out from the brush, knives in hand. One reached for the bridle of Jim's horse.

"No, you don't!" Jim cried, and drew his new knife from its leather sheath. He struck the man on the head and he fell, just as another of the three reached toward Bowie from the side. Jim kicked out at him and took the blow on the calf of his leg. In an instant he was off the horse and on his feet. One swing of the knife took care of this man, and the third one decided to run from this madman. Bowie stopped him with one more blow. This testing of the new knife brought it fame, and in a few years the "Bowie knife" was in use by woodsmen everywhere, and in the United States Army.

Jim was married to his Spanish-Mexican lady later that same year at San Antonio de Bexar. In 1833, the beautiful young wife and the two babies that had come to her and Jim died of cholera. Her father, who had given the young couple valuable mining land, also died. Jim Bowie, at thirty-seven, was very wealthy, but the meaning had gone from his life. Soon he was in the midst of the plans to bring freedom to Texas.

Off in Tennessee, the famous bear hunter and frontiersman Davy Crockett reached a decision. He was a little bitter over the fact that he had not been re-elected as a representative to Congress in the 1834 elections.

"There's a place for honest folk in Texas," Davy told his wife, Elizabeth. "And I think they could use Betsey and me to help make Texas free." So he shouldered Betsey, his trusty rifle, packed up his frontiersman's clothes, put on his good congress suit and boarded a steamboat to go west.

He went to Texas the long way around, going up the Arkansas River to Little Rock, and then down the Red River to Natchitoches. It was already late in the year of 1835 when he headed out on the trail to Texas. He found the "old Spanish Road" was still just a faint trail, often located only by following the blaze marks on the trees. He was traveling with a small party of other Tennessee men also heading for Texas. They reached Nacogdoches and found that beyond it the country opened out into grasslands.

Soon after they had crossed the Trinidad River, they heard a sound like thunder rumbling in the distance. But the sky was clear, and there were no signs of a coming storm. But in the west they could see a great cloud of dust. The dust thickened and the rumbling grew louder as they drew nearer to it.

"Buffalo! That's what it is," cried one of the men. "Head for that grove of trees!"

They had no sooner got into the shelter of the little grove of trees than the great herd reached them, led by a big black bull. Davy's fingers were itching to bring down that leader. He raised Betsey to his shoulder, aimed and fired. The big bull let out a great roar and stopped so suddenly that there was a pile-up of the great shaggy beasts for a moment or two until they started forward again. The slug from Davy's gun had not been heavy enough to bring death to the big buffalo.

The men reined in their horses, holding them under the trees while the herd swung around the grove. It was useless to try to speak above the great rumble. It was like a thousand bass drums all being pounded at once. Davy Crockett shouted something to his friends as the last of the animals went by, but no one could hear him. The old hunter in Davy couldn't just let those buffalo

go. He was riding a Texas mustang that he had traded for his travel-weary horse in Nacogdoches. Now he wheeled the little animal about, left the grove of trees, and was off to chase the herd.

"Catch up to them, boy," he said, as he dug his heels into the mustang's sides. The horse seemed pleased at the chance to run. He tried his best, but the speed of the buffalo was so great that he could not close the space between himself and the herd. For about two hours, Davy urged the tough little horse along, until finally the buffalo herd grew dim in the distance and the mustang was winded.

"No use backtracking," Davy decided when the horse was ready to go on. "We'll head due west and pick up the trail somewhere."

He rode along at a walk for a while, breaking his own trail through the grasslands and occasional groves of trees. He saw no sign that any other man had ever been there. Horse and rider moved slowly along. Then, as they were leaving a grove of trees, Davy saw a beautiful sight. Just ahead, quietly grazing, was a herd of about one hundred wild horses. He rode quietly into their midst.

The wild horses began circling around the once-wild

mustang and his rider. It was as if the little horse found himself once again with old friends. He turned his head from one horse to another, bit the neck of one playfully, and rubbed noses with another whose eyes seemed filled with curiosity. Then the mustang began to kick up his heels, joyfully. He kicked and pranced about, giving Davy a very rough ride.

"Stop that, boy!" Davy said, panting to catch his breath. Then he dug his heels into his steed's ribs and the mustang charged right through the herd. All the wild horses followed, heads up, tails and manes streaming.

On and on went horse and rider leading the wild herd. The mustang tossed his head as if to say, "You see, fellows, I haven't forgotten how to run!" And on and on they went. Davy leaned forward and held on, letting his horse set his own pace. From behind him, he could hear the pounding of many hooves.

For half an hour, Davy felt the rush of the wind over his head. He knew how the rider of a great racehorse must feel. Then his little mustang slowed, and a beautiful bay horse came alongside.

Davy spurred his steed on, as excited by the race as was his horse. Once again, but for just a moment, the mustang led the herd. Fast as he was, he could not carry the weight of a rider and hold the lead any longer. The bay passed him. So did a second wild horse and a third, and then the little mustang was back in the midst of the herd. He fell farther and farther back until the last of the wild horses had passed. Still he did not stop, but followed on until the herd reached the bank of a stream.

The leading horse leaped from the bank into the rushing water and then swam across. All the wild horses followed. Davy's horse reached the bank as the last of the herd climbed out of the water on the other side. The mustang stopped, stood still a moment, and then, as Davy was dismounting, suddenly lay down on the ground.

Davy unbuckled the straps and took the saddle, blanket, and reins from the horse. He rubbed the horse's leg muscles and his gleaming hide. The mustang lay panting. At last Davy felt he had done all he could for him. The horse still did not rise, so Davy spread the saddle blanket over him. The sun was setting by then, and it seemed that horse and rider would spend the night here on the bank of the stream. As Davy took cornmeal and dried meat from his saddle roll, the horse followed him with his eyes, with a look that plainly said,

"I have given my all for you."

Davy decided to sleep in the branches of a fallen tree, but found a cougar was there ahead of him. He fired old Betsey, but in the dark his aim was poor and he only stunned the wildcat. Before the battle for the roost in the tree was won, Davy had to slash again and again at the cougar with his knife. When at last the cat lay dead, he left it lying on the ground, too tired to skin it, and made himself a nest of branches in the tree. He fell asleep and did not awaken until daylight.

His first thought was of his sick horse. Would he be able to get up this morning? He climbed rather stiffly from his roost, and looked at the place where the horse had lain. No horse was there, nor was he anywhere in sight.

"He sure had me fooled," Davy muttered. "Well, now we are in a fix, off here in empty old Texas with no horse to carry us." He peered down the river a way and saw some wild geese. "Come on, Betsey," he said, taking aim with his gun, "at least we don't need to go hungry." Betsey answered in good form, and soon Davy was pulling feathers off a goose while his campfire burned to a proper point to cook the fowl.

"We'll do some pondering while we eat," he said

aloud. But the goose tasted so good to him that he let his thoughts stray instead of facing his problem. He had just finished eating when he heard the sound of horses coming.

"The wild herd again?" he wondered. "Not loud enough for buffalo."

In a moment he had his answer. A band of fifty Comanche Indians rode into view, divided into two groups, and surrounded him. "My goose is cooked in more ways than one," thought Davy. He had a firm grip on Betsey, but there was little use in trying to use the gun against this company. The chief got down from his horse and tried to pull the gun away from Davy.

"Are you at war with the Americans?" Davy asked.

"No," the chief replied.

Davy asked where the Indians got their rifles and knives and blankets. The chief admitted they were gifts from the United States.

"Then why rob me?" Davy asked. "I am an American."

The chief grunted and let go of Betsey. Davy explained how he happened to be in the wilderness alone, without a horse.

"Ha!" said the chief. "Mustang smart animal. He

pretend to be too sick to get up. We let you use horse."

Soon they were all riding on together. One of the squaws had skinned the wildcat, which looked as if some animal had had a good feast during the night, and she took the skin with her.

They had been riding about three hours when they came upon the herd of mustangs. One of the Indians got his rope ready to lasso a horse, riding ahead while the other Indians held back. All but one of the horses were away like wind as soon as they saw the Indian coming. The one who remained stood quietly and let himself be roped. It was Davy's mustang.

Before long, they were on the outskirts of the Austin colony. The Indians went no farther, and Davy rode on alone. At a river crossing, he found his traveling companions, camping for the night. As they journeyed on, others joined them, for the word had spread that fighting men were needed in San Antonio de Bexar.

The newcomers to Texas were eager to know what had been happening.

"Texas is free; and we want to keep it that way," they were told.

Davy and his friends learned that about seven months earlier, in June of 1835, a tall fellow with dark red hair,

William Barret Travis, had led a small company of Texans to a place near Galveston Bay where Santa Anna had stationed some soldiers. Travis' men had driven them out and taken the town. Then Santa Anna had decided Texas would have to have strong military government, so he sent his brother-in-law, General Martin Cos, to San Antonio to be military governor of Texas. With him came 1200 soldiers. They were quartered in the Alamo, the old mission-fort just outside the town.

The Texans decided they would not stand for military government, and volunteers gathered to try to drive General Cos out. First they went to Goliad, a town to the southeast of San Antonio, down near the Gulf of Mexico. Fifty men charged the fort there, led by old Ben Milam, tall, grizzled and weathered. Ben had come to Texas some years back to start a colony of his own. He hadn't been a very good manager, but everyone liked him. Ben and his fifty men had made the Mexican soldiers leave the fort and had taken all the guns and ammunition that they left and gone on up to Gonzales.

Gonzales was about fifty miles east of San Antonio. The Texas volunteers took the fort there, too, driving out about 150 Mexican soldiers.

"Now we'll get rid of General Cos and his army up at Bexar!" they cried. Led by Milam, Jim Bowie and Francis Johnson they moved up near San Antonio. Johnson was a surveyor who had come to Texas in 1826, and had risen to a government position in the Austin colony.

On December 4th, Ben Milam had stood before the men gathered around San Antonio de Bexar, raised his rifle high, and cried out, "Who'll follow old Ben Milam into Bexar?" The great shout that arose told Ben that the men were with him. They stormed the town, and on December 10, General Cos had surrendered.

"You should have seen us," some of the fighters told Davy Crockett and the other newcomers. "We got up on the roofs of the houses and picked off those soldiers like so many fish in a barrel! Five days and five nights we stormed that town, firing from behind walls and the rooftops until General Cos had to give up. Lost more than three hundred men, he did!"

About a dozen Texans had died in this battle. One of them was old Ben himself, after having earned a hero's place in the hearts of all the Texans.

General Cos had agreed that Texas had won its freedom. Then the Texans had ordered him to march his men back to Mexico City and tell Santa Anna. But

Santa Anna, it seems, had heard of what had happened at Goliad and Gonzales, and was already on his way to Texas with thousands of soldiers. General Cos met him and was ordered to turn back towards Texas and fight.

Before he heard this, Davy Crockett had decided he might just as well start choosing some farm land. "Looks like we're too late to help Texas win her freedom," he said.

"No, Davy, I think we're still going to need you," he was told. "Santa Anna is on his way back, and there aren't many men over there at San Antonio to stop him. Most of them went with Colonel Johnson back down to the coast. He and some of the others think we should march on down to Metamoros, beyond the Rio Grande, and get Santa Anna to come over that way.

"So Sam Houston sent Jim Bowie and a few volunteer soldiers to San Antonio and told him to blow up the old Alamo there. But the fellows who were there said that's where they should try to stop Santa Anna. Then Lieutenant Travis was sent there with twenty-five soldiers, and told to do the same thing. They had a scrap at first, and then decided to just send word for more men to come to Bexar, that they were going to stop Santa Anna there, in the old Alamo."

"Sounds like they'll need old Betsey and me and all you fellows," said Davy Crockett. "Time's a-wastin'! On to the Alamo!"

THE LONE STAR REPUBLIC OF TEXAS

High in the bell tower of San Fernando Church young Daniel William Cloud stood· watch. It was the highest place in San Antonio de Bexar, the best place from which to scan the countryside to make sure that Santa Anna's men were not marching toward the town.

The day was February 23, 1836, about two weeks after Davy Crockett and his Tennessee Mounted Volunteers had arrived. About one hundred fifty men altogether had answered the call for volunteers to come to defend the Alamo. So far, they hadn't done much drilling. Mostly they were just resting up and enjoying themselves in the town, not even going near the old mission-fort.

The day before had been George Washington's Birthday. All the Americans thought there should be a big celebration, even though Texas was not part of the United States. They held a big party—a *fandango*, they called it. And all the Mexicans had joined in the fun. Davy Crockett had made speeches half the afternoon and danced and played the fiddle half the night.

Seemed he was trying to prove that the fiddle made better dance music than the Mexicans' guitars, and most of the people had a big time dancing to both.

The fandango might have been going on yet if a messenger hadn't arrived sometime after midnight. He'd gone right to Jim Bowie. Then Jim had called out for everyone to be quiet.

"Got some bad news," he said. Then, before he could tell the suddenly silent crowd what his message had been, he began to cough. Jim was growing thinner and coughing more and more.

When he could speak again, Jim Bowie said, "We have word that may or may not be true. The message says that Santa Anna reached the Medina River, only eight miles from here, late on the 21st, and that his troops have been resting there all day today."

Lieutenant Travis shared command of the men at San Antonio. He was in charge of the regular soldiers. Bowie was in command of the volunteers.

"It can't be true," said Travis. "No one could move an army of men who have to be fed, not to mention horses and mules, across the desert in winter. It is somebody's idea of a joke, to send such a message."

Jim Bowie was not so sure. "We'd better close up this

fandango, anyway," he said. And the party had broken up.

Daniel had been ordered up into the tower to begin the watch about an hour after sunrise. He was growing tired of his job, and it was not yet ten o'clock. So far, for all his gazing out to the west and the southwest, he had seen nothing but the endless rolling land, nearly treeless. Looking down into the plaza and the streets, though, there had been more to see. Most of the Mexican families who lived in Bexar must have believed the message. All morning, their oxcarts, loaded with household belongings, had been creaking their way eastward. They were leaving town, and more and more of the houses had that silent, shuttered look that comes only when the people have left them, expecting to be away for a long time.

Daniel sat on the broad sill of the opening on the west side of the bell tower. His thoughts strayed. This might turn out to be the exciting time he had come to Texas to find. He had left his Kentucky home just a few months ago to go to St. Louis to open a law office. But he soon found that people did not beat a path to the door of an inexperienced young fellow when there were plenty of older lawyers around. So he had written his family that he was going to Texas to get in on the excitement there. He'd arrived in San Antonio de Bexar a month ago, and nothing had happened.

"Probably nothing will happen now, either," he said aloud. "Travis seemed so sure that Santa Anna couldn't get here until the middle of March, and that we'll have plenty of men here to hold the Alamo and the town by that time. He thinks those fellows who started for Matamoros will be sent back here. Seems Johnson changed his mind, but now the government is all split up, too, and the council has put a fellow named Fannin in charge of the men. Seems to me that the trouble with Texas right now is that there are too many men trying to be the boss. From what I hear, it would be better if Mr. Austin took charge. But they don't seem to want him anymore, and besides, he's gone to the United States to ask for help in Washington."

Daniel got up and paced about the bell tower for a moment. He looked out the east window. The sun was high in the sky now. It must be about ten o'clock. He moved back to the arched opening on the west side, and looked far out across the land. His eyes were blinded for a moment by the glint of sunshine striking polished steel.

He looked again, blinking his eyes to be sure of what he was seeing far off there on the horizon. He turned and took hold of the bell rope. He pulled and let go, and the bell broke the silence. He jumped and held onto the rope, pulling and then rising with the rope to pull again and again. The bell sent its call of alarm out across the town and to the countryside beyond. Daniel's eardrums felt as if they would burst, but he pulled again and again until the air was filled with the pealing of the bell, echoing and re-echoing, and meeting itself in all directions.

Daniel couldn't hear the pounding of footsteps as Lieutenant Travis came rushing to the top of the bell tower. He felt a rough hand on his shoulder, pulling him away from the rope, and a voice cut through the sound. "Enough, enough!" Travis was shouting. "If Santa Anna is within fifty miles, he'll have heard the bells and know we've seen him."

Another man arrived. He was Dr. John Sutherland, one of the six physicians who had volunteered for duty. "What did you see, boy?" he called out.

"Look!" said Daniel, pointing to the west. "Thousands of them!"

Travis and Sutherland peered out over the land,

shading their eyes to cut the glare.

"I see nothing but bare ground," said Travis.

"Bare ground and a few pools of water left from yesterday's rain," said Dr. Sutherland.

Others had arrived now and the little platform was crowded. All tried to see the cause of the alarm.

"The lad is seeing things! He let his imagination get ahead of his eyesight," Travis said.

Daniel rubbed his eyes and shook his head as if to free himself of some kind of veil. They had been there, he was sure of it! Men on horseback, men wearing helmets that shone in the sunshine. Now he could not see them either. Had he imagined it? No, he was sure of what he had seen.

"But I saw them! There must have been thousands of men," he insisted.

The men on the platform turned and began to go down the steep stairs. "Too much fandango last night," one said, and the others agreed.

Travis and Sutherland stayed. Travis studied the bare land in all directions. Much of it still showed the charring where the Texans had burnt off the grasses to help starve out Cos' men in October, but a little green was beginning to show. Could the boy have been right?

Could an army on horseback have come this far, in spite of the lack of spring grasses? But where were they now? He could see a low ridge or two off in the distance, and perhaps they had dropped below one of them. It would be wise to check.

"Stay on watch, Cloud, and this time see straight before you ring that bell," Travis said. He turned and went down the stairs, Sutherland following.

Many men had gathered in the plaza now. They were on foot, for their horses were grazing along a creek, five miles from town. Only two had their horses in town, Dr. Sutherland and a man named John W. Smith.

"You two ride out, just to make sure," Travis ordered Sutherland and Smith.

Dr. Sutherland remembered the puzzled look on Daniel's face. Maybe the lad had seen something after all. He turned to mount his horse.

"Tell the boy that if he sees us coming back full speed to start ringing that bell again," he said to Travis. Smith had also mounted his horse, and the two rode away.

Travis ordered the men to check supplies in the Alamo to make sure that they were ready, if an alarm was sounded again. He posted Crockett in the plaza to await the return of Sutherland and Smith. He sent the message up to Dan in the tower, and headed out towards the Alamo himself.

From the tower, Daniel watched the two riders head down the old trail. They disappeared in a little dip. Then he could see them again, riding toward the top of a rise. They reached the top, about a mile and a half from town. They stopped, motionless for a moment, and then wheeled about. In the quickness of the turn, Dr. Sutherland's horse stumbled, and the doctor fell. Dan saw Smith stop his horse, go back, and help the doctor back into the saddle. Then on they came, dropping into the dip, reappearing soon. They were galloping back as fast as their horses could bring them, as if Santa Anna himself were on their heels.

Daniel seized the bell rope and pulled. Again the alarm rang out, this time taken seriously by all who heard it. As the riders reached the edge of town, Dan hurried down from the tower, to join the others as they hastened out to the Alamo. There were a few families left in town, mostly those of the Mexicans who were fighting with the Americans, and now they hurried towards the fort. One American-Texan family went inside, too, the wife and baby daughter of Captain Almeron Dickinson.

The Alamo had thick stone and plaster walls, with the main part of it built around an open square. Workrooms and little houses lined the walls. There was also a long two-story building for housing soldiers, and the big church at one corner. The roof of the church had caved in, but most of its walls still stood, about twenty-two feet high and four feet thick. By noon, the whole place was a beehive of activity.

Sacks of corn were brought from the deserted huts outside the fort and some was found inside. A small herd of beef cattle was rounded up and brought inside the big square. The old water supply was opened and found to be in good condition, so food and water were on hand. Ammunition was more of a problem. Someone thought of using the lead from the old church window panels to make bullets, and this was done. Horseshoes and other pieces of scrap metal were broken up to load into cannon muzzles in place of cannonballs. The story of what happened inside those old walls in the next twelve days is a dramatic story of courage.

By three o'clock that afternoon, February 23, 1836, Santa Anna's men had arrived inside the town of Bexar.

A blood-red flag was flying from the church where Daniel Cloud had stood guard just that morning. "No quarter," was the message of that flag—Santa Anna would grant no mercy to any Texan captured. It was to be a fight to the end.

Lieutenant Travis wrote messages and sent them out, carried by Smith and Sutherland, to Gonzales, to Goliad, to any place from which help might come. He especially wanted Fannin to bring the hundreds of men up from the Gulf coast, and Travis' old friend, Jim Bonham, made a heroic ride to try to get them. They did not come, and after deciding to remain on the coast, were attacked and badly defeated by another part of Santa Anna's army.

On February 24, Travis sent his last call for help, in which he said, "I shall never surrender or retreat . . . . Victory or death." The next day, Jim Bowie was trying to help move a cannon on a platform fifteen feet above the ground. The cannon began to roll. With all his strength, Bowie brought it to a halt, but as other men held it and began to move it to a safe position, Bowie lost his balance and plunged to the ground. He was put on a cot, taken with great spasms of coughing, and within hours he lay feverish with pneumonia.

Spirits brightened a little on March 1, when the men had endured a rain of fire into the old mission-fort for seven days. Thirty-two men from Gonzales arrived, making their way into the Alamo by crawling through old irrigation ditches. Hopes were dashed two days later when Bonham returned to the Alamo, riding through enemy fire to get there, with word that Fannin was not coming.

All that day, Santa Anna's men had pounded the Alamo's walls with cannonballs. Some of the Mexican soldiers had set up scaling ladders to climb the Alamo walls. The men in the Alamo, many of them almost as expert with a rifle as Davy Crockett, had sent the attackers tumbling back. But it was clear that the bullet supply could not last much longer, nor would the weakened mission walls stand for many more days against the pounding of cannonballs.

Late in the afternoon of the day of Bonham's return, March 3, quiet came for a while. Travis, who had not yet told the men that Fannin's men were not coming, called for all the men to line up. Even Bowie was brought out into the open square on his cot. Travis stood before them then, and told them there was no hope of help.

"This is our certain doom," he said. "All that remains is to die in the fort and fight to the last moment. We must sell our lives as dearly as possible."

Then, it is said, he drew a line in the clay soil with his sword. "Each man who will stand with me to the end, come across this line," he said.

A minute later, of 183 men in all, only two were left on the other side of the line. One was Jim Bowie, on his cot. "Help me over, boys," he called, and four men quickly moved the cot across the line. The one man who was left was an older man who had suffered much in his youth in European wars. He left the fort that night.

On the night of March 5, the Alamo shook with the bombardment of the Mexican cannons. At five the next morning, the sound of bugles marked a great charge against the Alamo. Charge after charge was made, and the Mexican soldiers came pouring into the Alamo. William Travis was one of the first to die. Jim Bowie died, firing from his cot. Davy Crockett was found with Mexican soldiers in their blue and red uniforms heaped about him. By eight o'clock in the morning of that day, March 6, not one defender of the fort was alive.

Santa Anna's men found the women and children,

who had seen husbands and fathers die before their eyes, huddling inside the houses in fear. They questioned them and let all of them go except the American woman, Mrs. Dickinson. Santa Anna called her before him. Limping from a bullet in her leg, carrying her baby girl, Mrs. Dickinson went to his headquarters.

"You need not fear," Santa Anna told the trembling woman. "You will be well taken care of. You see, I want to adopt your little Angelina, your beautiful baby girl. She will have the best of everything in all the world."

Mrs. Dickinson could hardly believe her ears.

"Never!" she answered. "I will never give my baby to the man who killed her father!"

Nothing Santa Anna did or said would make Mrs. Dickinson change her mind. On March 13 she and her baby were released, given a horse and sent to Gonzales with the message from Santa Anna that all who did not lay down their arms would die.

The people there heard the message, but they also learned of the bravery of the 182 men in the Alamo. Who could hear of such courage and not be ready to fight on? When Sam Houston, who had been away at the time of the siege of the Alamo, called for volunteers, almost every able-bodied man answered the call. "Remember the Alamo!" became the battle cry, and they began to train for battle.

Santa Anna's men had swept from town to town, forcing all to retreat before him, until he reached Galveston Bay. Not far from present-day Houston, at San Jacinto, his men pitched their tents in a great camp, and the general called a halt for a celebration of victory.

It is said that a captured servant girl, knowing that Sam Houston was coming with four hundred men, made sure that General Santa Anna was enjoying himself in the camp so much that he did not realize what was happening until it was too late. General Houston planned his moves carefully, so that there would be no escape for the Mexican soldiers except into the swamps or the bay.

The Battle of San Jacinto began on April 18. Before it was over, on April 21, Sam Houston's big white horse had been shot from under him, and a bullet had pierced the general's ankle. He went on into battle on a little mustang, only to be brought down by another bullet.

"Remember the Alamo!" the men cried, and pressed on. Santa Anna found himself surrounded. Men in the rough clothes of the American frontiersman demanded that he place his signature on a paper that gave complete freedom to Texas. The surrender came very near to the place where the Spanish had first set foot on Texas soil three hundred years before.

That fall, General Sam Houston was elected the first president of the new Republic of Texas. People called it the "Lone Star Republic" because of the banner that flew over the capitol in Washington-on-the-Brazos. It was red and white with one big lone star on a field of blue. There were more years of struggle ahead before Texas became the twenty-eighth state of the United States in 1845, and the Lone Star Republic became the Lone Star State. Its people have never forgotten the heroes who made the lone star rise.